Abraham Lincoln

Abraham Lincoln

These and other titles are included in The Importance Of biography series:

Maya Angelou
Louis Armstrong
James Baldwin
Lucille Ball
The Beatles
Alexander Graham Bell
Napoleon Bonaparte
Julius Caesar
Rachel Carson
Charlie Chaplin
Charlemagne
Winston Churchill
Christopher Columbus
Leonardo da Vinci
James Dean
Charles Dickens
Walt Disney
Dr. Seuss
F. Scott Fitzgerald
Anne Frank
Benjamin Franklin
Mohandas Gandhi
John Glenn
Jane Goodall

Martha Graham
Lorraine Hansberry
Ernest Hemingway
Adolf Hitler
Thomas Jefferson
John F. Kennedy
Martin Luther King Jr.
Bruce Lee
John Lennon
Douglas MacArthur
Margaret Mead
Golda Meir
Mother Teresa
John Muir
Richard M. Nixon
Pablo Picasso
Edgar Allan Poe
Queen Elizabeth I
Jonas Salk
Margaret Sanger
William Shakespeare
Frank Sinatra
Tecumseh
Simon Wiesenthal

Abraham Lincoln

by Karen Marie Graves

LUCENT
BOOKS®

THOMSON

GALE

San Diego • Detroit • New York • San Francisco • Cleveland • New Haven, Conn. • Waterville, Maine • London • Munich

LIBRARY OF CONGRESS CATALOGING-IN-PUBLICATION DATA

Graves, Karen Marie.
    Abraham Lincoln / by Karen Marie Graves.
        p. cm. — (The importance of)
Includes bibliographical references and index.
Summary: Profiles the sixteenth president of the United States, whose life and
accomplishments were founded on his firm commitment to the words of the
Declaration of Independence.
    ISBN 1-56006-965-1 (hardback : alk. paper)
    1. Lincoln, Abraham, 1809–1865—Juvenile literature.   2. Presidents—United States—
Biography—Juvenile literature. [1. Lincoln, Abraham, 1809–1865. 2. Presidents.]
I. Title. II. Series.
    E457.905 .G73 2003
    973.7'092—dc21

                                                                                2001005524

Printed in the United States of America

Contents

Foreword

THE IMPORTANCE OF biography series deals with individuals who have made a unique contribution to history. The editors of the series have deliberately chosen to cast a wide net and include people from all fields of endeavor. Individuals from politics, music, art, literature, philosophy, science, sports, and religion are all represented. In addition, the editors did not restrict the series to individuals whose accomplishments have helped change the course of history. Of necessity, this criterion would have eliminated many whose contribution was great, though limited. Charles Darwin, for example, was responsible for radically altering the scientific view of the natural history of the world. His achievements continue to impact the study of science today. Others, such as Chief Joseph of the Nez Percé, played a pivotal role in the history of their own people. While Joseph's influence does not extend much beyond the Nez Percé, his nonviolent resistance to white expansion and his continuing role in protecting his tribe and his homeland remain an inspiration to all.

These biographies are more than factual chronicles. Each volume attempts to emphasize an individual's contributions both in his or her own time and for posterity. For example, the voyages of Christopher Columbus opened the way to European colonization of the New World. Unquestionably, his encounter with the New World brought monumental changes to both Europe and the Americas in his day. Today, however, the broader impact of Columbus's voyages is being critically scrutinized. *Christopher Columbus*, as well as every biography in The Importance Of series, includes and evaluates the most recent scholarship available on each subject.

Each author includes a wide variety of primary and secondary source quotations to document and substantiate his or her work. All quotes are footnoted to show readers exactly how and where biographers derive their information, as well as provide stepping stones to further research. These quotations enliven the text by giving readers eyewitness views of the life and times of each individual covered in The Importance Of series.

Finally, each volume is enhanced by photographs, bibliographies, chronologies, and comprehensive indexes. For both the casual reader and the student engaged in research, The Importance Of biographies will be a fascinating adventure into the lives of people who have helped shape humanity's past and present, and who will continue to shape its future.

IMPORTANT DATES IN THE LIFE OF ABRAHAM LINCOLN

1820
The Missouri Compromise is enacted.

1843
Robert Todd Lincoln is born on August 1.

1840
Lincoln is reelected to the Illinois legislature. Lincoln meets and becomes engaged to Mary Todd.

1809
Abraham Lincoln is born on February 12 in Kentucky.

1834
Lincoln is elected to the Illinois state legislature as a Whig.

1810	1820	1830	1840

1818
Lincoln's mother, Nancy, dies.

1832
Lincoln is defeated in run for Illinois House of Representatives, his first try for elective office.

1837
Lincoln moves to Springfield on April 15 and opens a law practice with John Stuart.

1819
Lincoln's father, Thomas, marries Sarah Bush Johnston.

1836
Lincoln obtains his license to practice law.

1842
Lincoln marries Mary Todd on November 4.

1850
Four-year-old Edward dies on February 1. Compromise of 1850 measures are enacted. William Wallace Lincoln is born December 21.

1859
Lincoln loses Senate race to Stephen Douglas.

1860
Lincoln is elected sixteenth president of the United States on November 7.

1853
Thomas (Tad) Lincoln is born on April 4.

1862
Eleven-year-old Willie dies on February 20. Lincoln reads draft of Emancipation Proclamation on July 22. Issues Emancipation Proclamation after winning Battle of Antietam on September 17.

1854
Congress passes the Kansas-Nebraska Act (which motivates Lincoln to action).

1857
Dred Scott decision by the U.S. Supreme Court.

1863
Lincoln signs the final Emancipation Proclamation on January 1.

1850	1855	1860	1865

1846
Edward Baker Lincoln is born March 10. Lincoln is elected to the United States House of Representatives.

1864
Lincoln is nominated for president by new (temporary) National Union Party. Lincoln wins reelection on November 8. Senate passes thirteenth Amendment, which outlaws slavery, in April.

1858
Lincoln wins Republican nomination for Senate, accepts with House Divided speech. Lincoln-Douglas debates.

1861
Lincoln is inaugurated on March 4. South Carolina, then Mississippi, Florida, Alabama, Georgia, and Louisiana secede in January; Confederacy is formed in February. The Civil War begins April 12 with firing on Fort Sumter.

1865
House ratifies thirteenth Amendment (ratified eight months after Lincoln's death). Lincoln is inaugurated March 4. General Robert E. Lee surrenders April 9. Lincoln is shot on April 14 and dies the following morning.

"The Struggle Should Be Maintained"

Abraham Lincoln went from the wilderness to the White House, capturing the American Dream along the way. He took that dream and made it his own, proving it could be done. He rose from humble origins—a dirt farm and log cabin—to the presidency of the United States of America. And he was essentially a self-made man. Self-educated, with less than a year's formal schooling, and self-motivated, he overcame obstacles and adversity his entire life to finally achieve—and to become a symbol of—the American Dream.

Lincoln eloquently described to a group of Union soldiers how the American Dream pertained to them and why it was worth fighting for:

> It is in order that each of you may have through this free Government which we have enjoyed, an open field and a fair chance for your industry, enterprise, and intelligence; that you may all have equal privileges in this race of life, with all its desirable human aspirations. It is for this the struggle should be maintained, that we may not lose our birthright. The nation is worth fighting for, to secure such an inestimable jewel.[1]

That jewel, or birthright, as encompassed in the Declaration of Independence, was the foundation for all that Lincoln believed in and the inspiration for all he accomplished.

In his rise from modest origins to the presidency of the United States, Abraham Lincoln made the American Dream his own.

THE SHEET ANCHOR OF OUR DEMOCRACY

In his preface to Lincoln On Democracy, *political analyst and former New York governor Mario Cuomo explains how the Declaration of Independence shaped Lincoln and was his guiding light:*

Above all, the theme that courses through so many letters, speeches and fragments, the great addresses and the simple greetings alike, is the unyielding commitment to the principles of our Declaration of Independence, what he calls the "sheet anchor" of our democracy. Lincoln talked about the Declaration as a stump campaigner, during the debates with Stephen Douglas, and again as president at Gettysburg. All people were created equal. All people had the right to enjoy the fruits of their own labor. All people shared the right to advance as far as their talents could take them. America, Lincoln believed, was a great society because it promised to "clear a path for all," to provide opportunity for anyone with skill and ambition. When the institution of slavery blocked that road, it was Lincoln who cleared the path. Some have since argued that he did it too slowly, or too halfheartedly, or too imprecisely. But the fact remains that it was he who did it. He saved our democracy. He improved our democracy. And he characterized our democracy in timeless words of inspiration for the benefit of all Americans who have followed.

It is not only Lincoln's words, eloquent as they are, that inspire us, but also his life and enormous accomplishments. Lincoln freed the slaves. He saved the nation. In the midst of chaos, tragedy, and overwhelming opposition, he remained true to his ideals.

The traits that helped to produce those accomplishments continue to inspire— and have become a fundamental part of U.S. history. His humanity, wit, and humor; his discipline, determination, and ambition; his generosity and humility all combine to make Lincoln so appealing. Yet in many ways he remains an enigma, even though more has been written about him than anyone, except perhaps Jesus and William Shakespeare.

Abraham Lincoln is generally recognized as the greatest U.S. president. Historians rank him first for his crisis leadership, vision, pursuit of justice, and administrative skills, and for these abilities alone his place in history would be secure. Stories of his personal devotion to the principles of democracy are known all over the world. But above and beyond all these things, Lincoln is at the center of the nation's self-image, which he helped to define, and in so doing changed the course of history.

1 A Simple, Poor Beginning

Abraham Lincoln was a seventh-generation American. Like many early American settlers, Lincoln's family originally came from Europe. Once in the United States, they moved many times in search of a better life. His great-great-great-great-grandfather, Samuel Lincoln, moved from Norfolk, England, to Hingham, Massachusetts, in 1637. The Lincoln family later migrated to Berks County, Pennsylvania. In the mid-1700s John Lincoln, Samuel's great-grandson and Abraham Lincoln's great-grandfather, moved to the Shenandoah Valley of Virginia. From there, Abraham Lincoln's grandfather Abraham, for whom he was named, moved the family to Kentucky in 1782. There, according to family legend, he was killed by American Indians while planting a cornfield with his six-year-old son, Thomas, who would later become the father of a president. Thomas had remained in the field beside his father's body and barely escaped the same fate. His older brother Mordecai, who had run to the cabin, saw through a crack in the logs that Thomas was also about to be killed and shot the would-be attacker as he approached the child.

MATERNAL ROOTS

Little is known about the Hankses, Lincoln's maternal ancestors. According to Lincoln, his mother, Nancy Hanks, was the illegitimate daughter of Lucy Hanks and a "well-bred Virginia farmer or planter." There is no record of the name of Nancy Hanks's father, but there is record in Mercer County (Kentucky) Court of a 1789 grand jury indictment (with no record of a trial) of a young woman named Lucy Hanks for loose and shameless conduct with men, lending credibility to Lincoln's account of his mother's illegitimacy. Nancy's mother Lucy, one of the few women of her time who could read and write, eventually married Henry Sparrow. Nancy was living with Sparrow's brother and sister-in-law, when in 1806, at twenty-two, she married Thomas Lincoln.

Abraham Lincoln was not particularly interested in his family history because he thought of himself as a self-made man. However, he attributed his ambition, analytical ability, and quick-wittedness to the genes inherited from the "unknown Virginian," qualities that he believed made him different from other family members and his peers. This mind-set could easily have been reinforced by his strong resemblance to his mother's side of the family. Although no portraits or drawings of Nancy Lincoln exist (and photography was not yet invented), she was said to be five feet ten inches tall, very tall for a woman of her generation, and rather lanky and athletic, as her son would prove to be. She was also described as strong-minded and intellectual, even brilliant. Thomas Lincoln, on the other hand, was of average height and stocky build. He was described as a plain, uneducated farmer, without pretensions or ambitions.

Whether Abraham Lincoln's greatness had its roots in a noble Virginia ancestor is impossible to say, but he began to distinguish himself as a young man, and perhaps his belief in his innate abilities gave him the confidence to persevere. Believing in those qualities most likely gave him a plausible explanation of why he grew up to be so different from his rather ordinary father.

When he was a young child, however, Lincoln did not differ greatly from his father or anyone else in the region. When asked for information to include in a proposed political biography for his first presidential campaign, he said:

> It is a great piece of folly to attempt to make anything out of my early life. It can all be condensed into a single sentence, and that sentence you will find in Gray's "Elegy": "The short and simple annals of the poor." That's my life, and that's all you or any one else can make of it.[2]

("Elegy Written in a Country Churchyard" by Thomas Gray was one of the most widely known poems of the early nineteenth century.)

POOR FARMER'S SON

The son of a dirt farmer, Abraham Lincoln's early life was poor and simple. On February 12, 1809, he was born in a one-room log cabin in Kentucky that, like most cabins in the area, measured about sixteen by eighteen feet, had a dirt floor, and no glass in the windows. He lived there with his mother, father, and older sister Sarah until he was almost two, when the family moved about ten miles away to a more fertile farm on Knob Creek. There, young Abraham helped his father to plant corn and pumpkins in the rich soil. He attended a "blab" school (so-called because the students recited their lessons aloud) with Sarah for brief periods, where he probably learned the alphabet. But he did not learn to read and write until after the family moved to Indiana in 1816, when Lincoln was seven.

The move was motivated partly by the difficulties with land titles in Kentucky at that time. But another reason—the source of what would ultimately become Lincoln's ideology—was his parents' opposition to slavery. Tom and Nancy Lincoln were Baptists, and they opposed slavery on religious and moral grounds as well as from an economic standpoint. (As a small farmer, Thomas Lincoln did not want to compete with slave labor.) Abraham grew up opposed to slavery, and in 1864, he commented, "I am naturally anti-slavery. If slavery is not wrong, nothing is wrong.

The son of a poor dirt farmer, Lincoln was born in this humble log cabin in Kentucky.

I can not remember when I did not so think, and feel."[3]

EARLY LIFE IN INDIANA

In Indiana, there were many other things that influenced Lincoln's development and character. Pigeon Creek, in the southwestern corner of the state near the Ohio River, was an unoccupied wilderness, heavily wooded, with bears, wolves, panthers, and other wild animals. Making matters worse, the family arrived during a harsh winter and lived in a three-sided pole shed that was exposed to the elements until, with the help of neighbors, they could build a log cabin. They had to keep a fire burning twenty-four hours a day for warmth. And to survive the winter, the family had to eat deer and bear meat, so someone had to hunt. Just before his eighth birthday, Abraham decided he would try to help. Seeing a flock of wild turkeys, he shot one. But killing the bird upset him terribly, and that was the first and last time he tried hunting.

That was not the case with other things Abraham tried. Before the Lincolns could plant corn, they had to clear away trees and underbrush, and the eight-year-old was asked to help his father clear the land: "Abraham, though very young, was large of his age, and had an ax put into his hands at once; and from that till within his twenty-third year he was almost con-

Autobiography: December 20, 1859

Lincoln was encouraged by a political supporter named J.W. Fell to write the following sketch, which was reprinted in many newspapers. This excerpt appears in Abraham Lincoln: His Speeches and Writings, *edited by Roy P. Basler:*

I was born February 12, 1809, in Hardin County, Kentucky. My parents were both born in Virginia, of undistinguished families—second families, perhaps I should say. My mother, who died in my tenth year, was of a family of the name of Hanks. . . . My paternal grandfather, Abraham Lincoln, emigrated from Rockingham County, Virginia, to Kentucky, about 1781 or 2, where, a year or two later, he was killed by indians, not in battle, but by stealth, when he was laboring to open a farm in the forest. His ancestors, who were Quakers, went to Virginia from Berks County, Pennsylvania. . . .

My father, at the death of his father, was but six years of age; and he grew up, litterally [sic] without education. He removed from Kentucky to what is now Spenser County, Indiana, in my eighth year. We reached our new home about the time the State came into the Union. It was a wild region, with many bears and other wild animals, still in the woods. There I grew up. There were some schools, so called; but no qualification was ever required of a teacher beyond "readin, writin, and cipherin." . . . Of course when I came of age I did not know that much. . . . I have not been to school since. The little advance I now have upon this store of education, I have picked up from time to time under the pressure of necessity.

I was raised to farm work, which I continued till I was twenty-two. At twenty-one I came to Illinois, and passed the first year in Macon County. Then I got to New Salem. . . . Then came the Black Hawk war; and I was elected Captain of Volunteers—a success which gave me more pleasure than any I have had since. I went . . . [through the entire military] campaign, was elated, ran for the Legislature the same year (1832) and was beaten. The next, and three succeeding biennial elections, I was elected to the Legislature. I was not a candidate afterwards. During this Legislative period I had studied law, and removed to Springfield to practise it. In 1846 I was once elected to the lower House of Congress. Was not a candidate for re-election. From 1849 to 1854, both inclusive, practiced law more assiduously than ever before. . . . What I have done since then is pretty well known.

A late nineteenth-century painting depicts Lincoln splitting rails, an image of him that endures to this day.

stantly handling that most useful instrument. . . ."[4] And so one of the most enduring, and endearing, images of Abraham Lincoln—the rail-splitter—was born. He continued to skillfully wield an ax and to thrive on the image that would later work to his advantage.

Another of Abraham's chores was to take corn to the mill to be ground into meal. One time Abe was late and in a hurry, and after he had hitched his horse to the arm of the gristmill (which turned the large stones that did the grinding), he used the whip to try to speed her up and grind the corn faster. She lashed out and kicked him in the head, and he was knocked unconscious. At first, it appeared that he was dead. His father was called to take him home. When Abe awoke, he could not speak for several hours, but when he did—illustrating his strong will and tenacity—he finished the sentence he had started before he was knocked out. And he suffered no permanent damage.

It was a constant battle against the elements, and Abraham Lincoln learned early that life is a struggle, and often a tragic one. When he was only nine his mother died of milk sickness, a disease contracted by drinking milk from a cow that had eaten poisonous white snakeroot. Young Abe helped his father to build the coffin by whittling the pinewood pegs that held it together.

Several years earlier Abe's infant brother had died, and later, his sister would die in childbirth. Life was difficult for most people living in newly settled areas at the time, with daily reminders of the uncertainty, frailty, and unfairness of existence. But if Lincoln's early experiences were typical, his reaction was not. Many experts believe that Lincoln's early struggles and losses, particularly the death of his beloved mother, were the root of his fatalistic outlook and the beginning of the periodic bouts of depression that he battled as long as he lived.

BELOVED STEPMOTHER

Within a year of Nancy Lincoln's death, Thomas Lincoln married Sarah Bush

Johnston, an old friend, who had been recently widowed. His new wife added three children by her first husband (Sarah Elizabeth, thirteen; Matilda, ten; and John D. Johnston, nine) to the family, which now included Nancy's cousin Dennis Hanks. The second Mrs. Lincoln was a positive force in young Abraham's life, by being supportive and encouraging. Although she was illiterate, she understood the importance of education. Lincoln called her "Mama," and felt nothing but affection for her. A relative remembered, "She had been his best friend in this world and no man could love a mother more than he loved her."[5] She felt the same toward him and recognized something special in him from the start. Years later in an interview, her admiration and affection for him were obvious as she described him:

> Abe was a good boy. He didn't like physical labor—was diligent for knowledge—wished to know and if pains and labor would get it he was sure to get it. He was the best boy I ever saw. . . . Abe never gave me a cross word or look and never refused in fact, or even in appearance, to do any thing I requested him. . . . He never told me a lie in his life—never evaded—never equivocated never dodged—nor turned a corner to avoid any chastisement or other responsibility.[6]

AN AVID READER

Although Lincoln had little formal schooling, he did acquire the skills necessary to educate himself. Through repetition and drill, he learned the rudiments of spelling, before becoming a proficient speller. And he learned to write well also—so well, in fact, that neighbors often asked him to write letters for them. But reading made the real difference. It opened the door for Lincoln and started him down the road that, when combined with his extraordinary determination, would increasingly distinguish him from other people.

Once he learned to read, he wanted to do it all the time. Books were scarce, but he read everything he could get his hands

Although he lacked a formal education, Lincoln was passionate about reading.

on. Lincoln often took a book along when he went to work so that he could read while he rested. When he returned from working, he would grab a piece of cornbread and a book and read some more.

Years later, cousin Dennis Hanks gave a vivid description of Lincoln's reading habits, indicating both how bizarre the behavior seemed to others and the confidence Sarah Lincoln placed in her stepson:

> I never seen Abe after he was twelve [that] he didn't have a book some'ers 'round. He'd put a book inside [h]is shirt an' fill his pants pockets with corn dodgers [small loaves of corn bread], an' go off to plow or hoe. When noon come he'd set down under a tree, an' read an' eat. In the house at night, he'd tilt a cheer [chair] by the chimbly [chimney] an' set on his backbone an' read. I've seen a feller come in an' look at him, Abe not knowin' nobody was 'round, an' sneak out agin like a cat, an' say, "Well, I'll be darned." It didn't seem natural, nohow, to see a feller read like that. Aunt Sairy's [Sarah] never let the children pester him. She always said Abe was goin' to be a great man some day. An' she wasn't goin' to have him hendered [hindered].[7]

The books the youthful Lincoln read, particularly those he read over and over, had a profound influence on him. At first, they were the books available to him. Some, such as those his stepmother had brought with her, had a strong moral component: the Bible, of course, and *The Pilgrim's Progress*, a very popular seventeenth-century novel of destruction followed by redemption. Not only the moral content of these books but also the rhythmic patterns of the prose later influenced some of his speeches. Lincoln read *Aesop's Fables* so many times that he knew them by heart. His favorite tale, "The Lion and Four Bulls" (or a variation, "The Lion and Four Oxen") reinforced the biblical passage that "a house divided against itself cannot stand," which found its way into one of his most important speeches. He also studied William Grimshaw's *History of the United States* and Parson Mason Weems's *Life of George Washington*, which impressed him with the hardships and struggles Washington had to endure.

Lincoln read methodically and memorized much of what he read. If he came across a passage he wanted to remember, he would write it down. Then he would rewrite it, look at it, and repeat it until he had it memorized. Once a text was committed to memory, Lincoln could recall it at any time, even years later.

STORYTELLER AND JOKER EARLY ON

In school, Lincoln's intelligence also set him apart, and that difference was soon apparent to him. He differed from his classmates physically, as well. Already taller than most of the students, and wearing a coonskin cap and buckskin pants that were so short six inches of his shin showed, Lincoln could not go unnoticed.

"HE WAS A CONSTANT AND VORACIOUS READER"

John Hanks was one of Lincoln's cousins and lived with the Lincoln family in their Indiana cabin for four years. When the boys were young, they were quite close. Hanks worked alongside the future president on the farm and went with him in a flatboat down the Mississippi in 1831.

In 1860 Hanks carried some log rails into an Illinois political meeting and claimed they had been split by Lincoln when he was young. His show-and-tell helped to spread the legend of Lincoln the rail-splitter and to fuel Lincoln's frontiersman image, lending momentum to his campaign.

This excerpt, as quoted in Lincoln: As I Knew Him, *edited by Harold Holzer, comes from recollections told to Lincoln's law partner and biographer, William Herndon, in June 1865, when Herndon was in the early stages of researching a biography of his recently assassinated friend.*

An artist's depiction of Lincoln and his step-mother studying together by firelight.

When Lincoln, Abe and I, returned to the house from work, he would go to the cupboard, snatch a piece of corn bread, take down a book, sit down on a chair, cock his legs up as high as his head, and read. He and I worked barefooted—grubbed it, plowed, mowed, and cradled together, plowed corn, gathered and shucked corn. Abraham read constantly when he had an opportunity—no newspapers then. . . . I know he read Weems' [Life of] Washington when I was there—[and] got it wet. It was on a kind of book shelf close to the window. The book shelf was made by two pins in the wall and a clap board on them, books on that. Lincoln got it of [from] [Josiah] Crawford [a neighbor], told Crawford [that he had ruined the book] and paid it in pulling fodder by two or three days' work. He frequently read the *Bible.* He read *Robinson Crusoe,* Bunyan's *Pilgrim's Progress.* Lincoln devoured all the books he could get or lay hands on: He was a constant and voracious reader.

But the other students were drawn to his jokes and storytelling as well as his quick wit. In *Lincoln*, David Herbert Donald describes how Lincoln's classmates reacted to him and how that experience helped to shape him:

> Unconscious of his peculiar appearance, he would rapidly gather the other students around him, cracking jokes, telling stories, making plans. Almost from the beginning he took his place as a leader. In their eyes he was clearly exceptional, and he carried away from his brief schooling the self-confidence of a man who has never met his intellectual equal.[8]

DIFFICULTIES WITH DAD

Like many adolescents, Lincoln grew increasingly distant from his father, and indeed, the two were very different personalities. Thomas was a simple man and uneducated. Although he encouraged Abraham to go to school, he did not truly understand what an education was. According to Dennis Hanks, Thomas thought Abraham spent too much time with his books and "sometimes had to slash him [with a strap] for neglecting his work by reading."[9] And as Abraham continued to grow—by age sixteen he was more than six feet two inches tall— Thomas increasingly depended on him to

---

THE FOUR OXEN AND THE LION

Lincoln was particularly fond of Aesop's Fables (sixth century B.C.), short, often humorous tales that teach a moral lesson. One of his favorites, according to David Herbert Donald, was "The Lion and the Four Bulls," a popular variation at the time of "The Four Oxen and the Lion." This translation from the original Greek is from The Harvard Classics *(1909–14).*

A Lion used to prowl about a field in which Four Oxen used to dwell. Many a time he tried to attack them; but whenever he came near they turned their tails to one another, so that whichever way he approached them he was met by the horns of one of them. At last, however, they fell a-quarrelling among themselves, and each went off to pasture alone in a separate corner of the field. Then the Lion attacked them one by one and soon made an end of all four.

"UNITED WE STAND, DIVIDED WE FALL."

This moral reprises the biblical passage, "And if a house be divided against itself, that house cannot stand" (Mark 3:25, King James version) that Lincoln undoubtedly knew first. It later found its way into one of his most important speeches, "A House Divided," delivered at the close of the Republican Convention (June 16, 1858), where he was nominated for the U.S. Senate to run against incumbent Stephen A. Douglas.

At nineteen, Lincoln saw a slave market for the first time when he visited New Orleans, and was horrified by the experience.

help with the heavy chores, even hiring him out to other farmers to hoe, split rails, or build fences. Thomas was hard working, a plodder, whereas Abraham was inclined to avoid physical labor whenever he could. Because he was growing so quickly, Abe was always tired, so he appeared lazy to many. And, of course, he was always reading or writing. But the real difference—and on this father and son were worlds apart—was ambition. As an adult, Lincoln remarked that his father "never did more in the way of writing than to bunglingly sign his own name,"[10] and that he chose to live where "there was absolutely nothing to excite ambition for education."[11] Because he was unable to understand why Thomas did not want to learn more, do more, or be more, Abraham did not want to be like his father.

VENTURING OUT

When Lincoln was nineteen, he had the opportunity to earn some money and venture farther from home when he helped a local merchant's son take a cargo by flatboat down the Mississippi River to New Orleans. This was the first time Lincoln had been to a big city, and he found it enlightening, stimulating, and probably a little overwhelming. It was also the first time he had seen a large number of slaves and a slave market. Before that, his opposition to slavery had been theoretical. In New Orleans, he saw human beings bought and sold like cattle. It horrified him and intensified his anti-slavery position.

Two years after the flatboat trip, in 1830, Lincoln helped his father to move the family to Macon County, Illinois. The two men had little to do with each other after that. Knowing only that he did not want to do farming and carpentry like his father, Lincoln had no idea how he would support himself. He was already leaning toward politics, though. In Decatur, Illinois, Lincoln gave his first political speech at a campaign meeting. It was spontaneous, in response to statements by established politicians, and the issue—improving the Sangamon River for transportation—was one of local rather than national importance. The future president had taken the first step on his own, and with nothing else to do, he followed up his first political speech by agreeing to take a flatboat of supplies to New Orleans for a rather unscrupulous entrepreneur named Denton Offutt.

2 Entering Politics

For the next six years, Lincoln lived in New Salem, Illinois. He was forced to stop there when his flatboat got stuck in the pond of the village mill. Although he was unable to dislodge the boat, Lincoln figured out a way to save the cargo. Local residents watched his efforts and admired the young boatman's ingenuity and tenacity. Their admiration grew as they watched him take on odd jobs to support himself while waiting for Denton Offutt to make good on his promise to open a store for Lincoln to manage.

GAINING FAVOR AND POPULARITY

Lincoln also gained favor by performing well in a now-legendary wrestling match. Wrestling was a popular frontier pastime for testing a person's skill, strength, and courage. Because of his size, strength, and determination, Lincoln excelled at the sport. When word of his prowess spread to nearby Clary's Grove, a group of local mischief-makers challenged Lincoln to a match with their leader and champion, Jack Armstrong. There are several versions of the event depending on the story-teller: In some versions Lincoln wins the match and in some Armstrong wins; in some Armstrong cheats or tricks Lincoln. But all versions have Lincoln coming out ahead in the end because, through his strength, courage, and good humor, he gained the respect of Armstrong and the Clary's Grove Boys and won the hearts of the townspeople. And he gained loyal friends who later helped him politically. Some historians view this incident as the turning point in Lincoln's life because of the support and position in the community he gained, which gave him a foothold for his entry into politics.

Lincoln's skill as a teller of anecdotes also helped him to gain acceptance and popularity. He quickly became a favorite at the general store where the men gathered to talk and hear the latest news. He never failed to entertain them with his wit and amusing stories, which he related with energy and enthusiasm. Belying the solemn expression usually seen in portraits and photographs made during his presidency, a contemporary described Lincoln telling a story in the following manner:

> . . . His countenance would brighten up, the expression would light up not

in a flash but rapidly, the muscles would begin to contract. Several wrinkles would diverge from the inner corners of his eyes, and extend down and diagonally across his nose, his eyes would sparkle, all terminating in an unrestrained laugh in which everyone present willing or unwilling were compelled to take part.[12]

Lincoln possessed other traits that endeared him to his newfound friends and commanded their respect. He was kind, considerate, and honest. And he was exceptionally eager to learn. He threw himself into any task or endeavor and stayed with it until he mastered it. He was fascinated with the law and the legal system and would often attend sessions of the local court. After a while, because his anecdotes added a little humor, the justice allowed him to informally address the court. But it was soon apparent that he also had a sharp, logical mind. Although he was not yet an attorney and had barely a year of formal schooling, New Salemites began to come to him for legal advice and for drafting simple legal documents. And those watching him closely were convinced he was headed for success.

Entering Politics

In March 1832 Lincoln announced his candidacy for the Illinois House of Represen-

People familiar with Lincoln's character felt certain that he was destined for success.

To the People of Sangamon County: Political Announcement March 9, 1832

Abraham Lincoln began his first political campaign by announcing his candidacy in Springfield's Sangamo Journal. *At twenty-three, with virtually no formal education and no political experience, and lacking the support of any influential politicians, he appealed directly to the public with a long, formal, rather pretentious statement. The opening and closing paragraphs are reprinted here from* Abraham Lincoln: His Speeches and Writings:

Fellow Citizens:

Having become a candidate for the honorable office of one of your representatives in the next General Assembly of this state, in accordance with an established custom, and the principles of true republicanism, it becomes my duty to make known to you—the people whom I propose to represent—my sentiments with regard to local affairs.

Every man is said to have his peculiar ambition. Whether it be true or not, I can say for one that I have no other so great as that of being truly esteemed of my fellow men, by rendering myself worthy of their esteem. How far I shall succeed in gratifying this ambition, is yet to be developed. I am young and unknown to many of you. I was born and have ever remained in the most humble walks of life. I have no wealthy or popular relations to recommend me. My case is thrown exclusively upon the independent voters of this county, and if elected they will have conferred a favor upon me, for which I shall be unremitting in my labors to compensate. But if the good people in their wisdom shall see fit to keep me in the background, I have been too familiar with disappointments to be very much chagrined.

Your friend and fellow citizen

A. Lincoln

New Salem, March 9, 1832

tatives. His official entry into politics revealed two recurring and seemingly contradictory traits: his self-confidence, shown by his entering the race at age twenty-three with no political experience, only a year of formal education, and no name recognition outside his immediate community; and his humility, shown by his announcement that how well he would succeed was "yet to be developed." In addition to humility—at least thirty-five times before 1860 he referred to himself as "humble"—Lincoln revealed much about himself and his future actions, decisions, and motivation in his declaration that his ambition was "no other so great as that of being truly esteemed of my fellow men, by rendering myself worthy of their esteem."[13]

Lincoln's first platform, printed in the local newspaper, was effective. His main thrust was an argument for the improvement of the Sangamon River for navigation. He also supported emphasizing education (but offered no plan or program) and a law against usury, the lending of money at high interest rates. It was well written because Lincoln had, with characteristic diligence, studied grammar to prepare for his run. More significant was how early in his political career he was incorporating his fundamental belief that opportunity and self-determination are essential elements of democracy.

BLACK HAWK WAR

Offutt's business ventures eventually failed. Lincoln, who was left without a job, enlisted in the militia for the Black Hawk War. This small-scale conflict was the response of Illinois settlers to attempts by Sauk and Fox Indians, under the leadership of Black Hawk, to reclaim the homeland that had been taken from them in an earlier treaty. In the volunteer militia, Lincoln met many of the men who would become influential and helpful to him in Illinois, including his future law partner, John T. Stuart. The men elected Lincoln captain, and in 1859, on the brink of national prominence, he cited this distinction as "a success which gave me more pleasure than any I have had since."[14] Unfortunately, he returned home

too late to effectively campaign for office. Because he was young and relatively unknown, he came in eighth out of thirteen in a race to elect four representatives. It was, as he would later point out with pride, the only time he "was ever beaten on a direct vote of the people."[15] It was actually an impressive debut. As Stuart observed,

> Lincoln in this race, although he was defeated, acquired a reputation for candor and honesty, as well as for ability in speech making. He made friends everywhere he went . . . and thereby acquired the respect and confidence of everybody.[16]

And he did receive the majority of votes from his precinct, which gave him a good start for the next election.

ENTREPRENEUR

Lincoln needed to find a way to support himself, so he went into partnership on a general store with William Berry, a former corporal in his company during the Black Hawk War. Business was slow, which gave Lincoln the opportunity to read—probably more than he had ever before been able to. He did not like fiction, but he memorized Shakespeare and some of the poetry that moved him, particularly verses by Scottish poet Robert Burns. His main interest was grammar—the structure and use of language—which he decided he needed to learn. When Lincoln learned that a farmer had a copy of Samuel Kirkham's *English Grammar*, con-

Lincoln's partnership in a general store afforded him time to read when he was not waiting on customers.

sidered the best instruction at the time, he walked six miles to borrow it. Then he methodically mastered the contents, demonstrating once again his determination and intelligence.

POSTMASTER AND SURVEYOR

The general store was forced to close, leaving the partners deeply in debt. Lincoln was once again unemployed. For a while, he returned to temporary jobs such as splitting rails and serving on juries. He did not want to leave New Salem, and

anxious to keep the promising young man around, his friends arranged to have him appointed village postmaster. That position provided him with the opportunity to read all the newspapers that came in and to visit with the residents, allowing him to develop further his talent as a storyteller, one of his most distinctive and memorable characteristics, and one essential to his political future. It helped him to become accepted and admired by future voters and to hone his verbal skills and make the most of his wit, which was good practice for future performing and public speaking. But the position paid little, and once again, his friends came through, this time helping him to secure an appointment as assistant surveyor. The new job would take him to all parts of the surrounding country, enabling him to become acquainted with many residents. Lincoln knew nothing about surveying, so he bought a compass and measuring chain, obtained the necessary books, and learned trigonometry and its application to surveying in six weeks. With the two positions, he earned barely enough to live on.

Then the Sangamon County Circuit Court issued a judgment against him and Berry for the overdue notes on their store. Because they could not pay in cash, the sheriff took personal possessions including Lincoln's horse, saddle, bridle, and surveying equipment, thereby depriving him of his means of livelihood. So, partially to help alleviate his financial problems, Lincoln ran for the state legislature again in 1834.

1834 STATE LEGISLATURE

In this campaign, Lincoln did not publish speeches or issue position statements, even though he strongly supported the policies of the Whig Party, a new political organization that would enjoy a brief period of prominence on the national scene. Instead, he met and greeted voters personally wherever he went. This was a calculated political move. Although New Salem was strongly Whig, the surrounding self-sufficient farmers belonged to the dominant Democratic Party. Many, in-cluding the loyal Clary's Grove Boys, supported Lincoln personally, despite their differing political views. They even threatened to withhold their support for the Democratic candidates for other offices if their fellow party members in surrounding counties did not help to elect Lincoln. As a result a deal was made that helped Lincoln to win the election.

In a field of thirteen candidates running for four seats, Lincoln was elected on August 4, 1834, with the second highest number of votes. To prepare himself for his first session in the Illinois state legislature, he studied law. He also wanted to make a proper appearance, so he borrowed money to buy the first suit he had ever owned.

His first term was uneventful; he mainly observed and learned from the more experienced members. But as the session progressed, his skill in drawing up legislation and mastery of the technical language grew. Other members increasingly asked him to draft bills for them.

STUDYING LAW

After the first session, Lincoln spent most of his time studying law during the spring and summer of 1835. He memorized, rephrased in his own words, and wrote down entire pages to remember the arguments. As his cousin Dennis Hanks remembered, "One thing is true of him . . . he was ambitious and determined and when he attempted to Excel by man or boy his whole soul and his Energies were bent on doing it."[17]

THE WHIG PARTY

The Whig Party (1834–1856) was formed to oppose Andrew Jackson, who was president from 1829 to 1837. Many, including Abraham Lincoln, who started his political career as a Whig, opposed the increasing strength, or what they considered executive tyranny, of "King Andrew." Led by Henry Clay of Kentucky, Whigs advocated strong federal support of the nation's economic development. Clay's American System (which drew on Alexander Hamilton's Federalist economic policy of 1791) called for federally subsidized roads and canals, a strong national bank, and a high tariff to protect American manufacturers.

In 1840 Whig candidate William Henry Harrison, a war hero, won the presidency with a campaign portraying him as a humble "log cabin" candidate of the people. When he died unexpectedly in 1841, Vice President John Tyler became president, vetoed the Whig program, and was expelled from the party. Henry Clay was the presidential candidate in 1844, but he lost when he opposed the annexation of Texas and lost support in the South. And the party began to split on the slavery issue, with the "Conscience" Whigs opposed to slavery and the "Cotton" Whigs favoring it. In 1848 General Zachary Taylor, another military hero, won the presidency for the Whigs, but he, too, died in office after serving only briefly. Soon after Taylor's death, Henry Clay, then a U.S. Senator, became a major architect of the series of legislative measures known as the Compromise of 1850, which offended the Conscience Whigs because it included a stronger Fugitive Slave Law. So in 1852, General Winfield Scott, yet another military hero, and the last Whig presidential candidate, was defeated by Franklin Pierce. Controversy over the proslavery Kansas-Nebraska Act in 1854 caused the breakup of the party. Many of the Conscience Whigs helped to form the new Republican Party (1854–1856 first time on presidential ballot), with others later following, while most Cotton Whigs joined the Democrats.

Lincoln had wanted to become a lawyer long before actually committing himself to a career at the bar. Although learning had previously appeared effortless for him, he became completely engrossed when he began to seriously study law. He read and studied so much that his friends worried about him; some thought the hard mental work injurious to his health, particularly when they noticed his mood changes and how he sometimes became gloomy and withdrawn.

ANN RUTLEDGE

It was during this time that he met and fell in love with Ann Rutledge, a bright,

STUDIOUS IN NEW SALEM

Abraham Lincoln was, in the truest sense and against enormous odds, a self-made man. In Honor's Voice, *Douglas Wilson explained how difficult and unusual was Lincoln's pursuit of law in New Salem:*

Like several others, [law partner, friend, and biographer Will] Herndon and [Illinois governor Joseph] Duncan remember that one of the lawbooks Lincoln read early in his New Salem years was Blackstone. Sir William Blackstone's *Commentaries on the Laws of England* (1765) was the most famous legal treatise of its time. . . . Though it was highly praised for its lucidity and graceful literary style, its vocabulary and intellectual presuppositions, to say nothing of its massive bulk, are still imposing for the uninitiated and must have been truly formidable for a self-educated frontiersman, whose only aid was a pocket dictionary. . . .

. . . Unlike Springfield, which attracted well-educated, propertied, and professional people, New Salem and environs were mainly settled by a relatively poor class of farmers, merchants, and tradesmen. There were no lawyers and, except for a few physicians, no professionally trained persons of any kind. The reputation of Lincoln's neighbors was that they were "rough," a term that probably relates to background as well as behavior, Lincoln being no exception. . . . In these circumstances, his decision to study law was somewhat anomalous [unusual], and the spectacle of the young Lincoln, "barefooted seated in the shade of a tree," plowing through a treatise such as Blackstone, was for the residents of New Salem a bizarre sight.

Lincoln's study of the law was considered unusual by the largely uneducated townspeople of New Salem.

pretty, good-hearted daughter of a tavern owner. In the midst of his studying—and in spite of a shyness and awkwardness with women that never left him—the couple came to an understanding and agreed to wait a year, until Lincoln was admitted to the bar, before marrying. Unfortunately, she became ill with what was known as brain fever (probably typhoid) and died on August 25, 1835. Lincoln was so devastated that it was difficult for him to function normally. Some of his friends worried that he was suicidal and convinced him to stay with a friend for a few weeks to rest and recuperate.

Some who knew him at the time thought Lincoln's extreme studiousness coupled with yet another premature death of one he dearly loved had caused temporary mental derangement. But others believed he became more engrossed in his law studies as a way to deal with his grief. This dedication may have helped him through his depression, much as years later his dedication as president of the United States during the Civil War would help him to cope with the death of his son Willie.

1836 State Legislature Campaign

Lincoln kept himself busy as a surveyor, politician, and law student. At that time, though law schools did exist, it was neither unusual nor an impediment for a lawyer to be self-educated like Lincoln. All that was necessary was to pass the bar exam. In March 1836, Lincoln took his first step toward admission to the bar

when, as was customary at the time, the Sangamon Circuit Court recorded him as a person of good moral character. In June he announced his candidacy for the legislature in the *Sangamo Journal*. He declared publicly his intention to vote for the Whig Party's presidential candidate, Hugh L. White, thereby aligning himself more closely with the party. And in agreement with Whig policy, he favored state support for internal improvements and the "doctrine of instructions," the belief that an elected representative is obligated to be governed by the will of his constituents and to act in their best interest.

It was a difficult campaign, traveling by horseback to public meetings in villages and hamlets, but Lincoln's diligence, skill as a speaker, and popularity paid off. In August, he received the most votes of the seventeen candidates. But he did lose the support of some of his rural friends and neighbors who were Democrats.

"Long Nine" Whig Delegation

In September Lincoln passed his bar examination and received his license to practice law in Illinois. When he went to the legislature, he was the Whig floor leader. As one of the "Long Nine" (the Whig delegation from Sangamon County, so-called because they were all tall), his primary objective was to relocate the capital of Illinois from Vandalia to Springfield. His first long speech in the legislature, which improved his standing and his image, brilliantly exposed the flaws in a resolution that Lincoln believed constituted a diversionary tactic on the part of an opponent of the relocation.

Also, Lincoln was one of six legislators who voted against a resolution condemning abolitionist societies. He entered a protest into the record, making his first public statement about the institution he abhorred:

> Resolutions upon the subject of domestic slavery having passed both branches of the General Assembly at its present session, the undersigned hereby protest against the passage of the same.
>
> They believe that the institution of slavery is founded on both injustice and bad policy; but that the promulgation of abolition doctrines tends rather to increase than to abate its evils.
>
> They believe that the Congress of the United States has no power, under the Constitution, to interfere with the institution of slavery in the United States.
>
> They believe that the Congress of the United States has the power, under the Constitution to abolish slavery in the District of Columbia, but that power ought not to be exercised unless at the request of the people of the District.[18]

Ultimately, Lincoln and the Long Nine shepherded through the bill to relocate the capital to Springfield. And Lincoln relocated to Springfield as well, where he went into partnership with John Stuart, an early political ally, to open a law office.

3 From Springfield to Washington

Lincoln considered the practice of law secondary to his political career, but he gained considerable legal experience and honed his skills as an attorney when he moved to Springfield and was in partnership with John Stuart. He also gained confidence in his abilities and unconventional training. Although he was essentially self-taught, when he compared himself with other attorneys he was their equal. When Stuart left to serve in Congress in 1839, Lincoln competently ran the office, writing in the fee book, "Commencement of Lincoln's administration." The firm was quite successful, despite his inclination to stuff paperwork in drawers, in his pockets, and especially in his stovepipe hat.

LEADER OF WHIGS IN STATE LEGISLATURE

As the leader of the Whigs in the state legislature, Lincoln was active in organizing the party and became one of the best-known Whigs in the state. He worked to establish Springfield as a town and to acquire funds to complete the new statehouse. He also continued to fight for a

plan to build a network of railroads and canals across the state, although an economic downturn and national financial panic in 1837 prevented its passage at that time. In a special legislative session, he voted with the majority to continue the improvements in spite of the panic.

Lincoln was reelected in 1838, having received the most votes of the seven winning candidates. He had become concerned about increasing lawlessness and social disorder after nationwide incidents of mob violence that included the vigilante execution of gamblers in Mississippi, the burning to death of a man accused of murder in St. Louis, lynchings in the South, and the murder of Elijah P. Lovejoy, editor of an abolitionist newspaper. Lincoln delivered a speech to the Young Men's Lyceum in which he called for reverence for the laws to become the "political religion of the nation."[19] He also appealed for increased reason and subdued passion.

ADJUSTING TO SPRINGFIELD

Despite his successes, both as a speaker and in public office, Lincoln's bouts with depression became more evident and more of a concern to his friends. The move to Springfield had been a difficult adjustment for Lincoln because he was in a new and different social setting. New Salem was a small frontier village where Lincoln had made a special place for himself and was accepted, admired, and respected. Springfield was larger, about fifteen hundred people, and had a more sophisticated social structure with a prominent group of refined, educated, privileged residents. With Lincoln's gawky appearance, awkward dress, and countrified speech, he did not fit in, and it would take more than a

Although successful as a politician and skilled in public speaking, Lincoln experienced episodes of depression.

wrestling match to establish himself in the state capital. As in New Salem, it was with men that Lincoln first made progress socially, and in time became quite popular with them. They enjoyed his amusing stories and admired his strength and athletic ability. And he related well to children because he felt comfortable with them. He was always there to lend a hand, and he was known for taking the children of the neighborhood to the circus. But Lincoln felt particularly inept when it came to relating to women.

In *Honor's Voice*, historian Douglas L. Wilson explained:

> What it comes down to, perhaps, is that Lincoln was simply ill at ease in polite society. Unaccustomed to its proprieties, he probably found the prescribed forms and manners an awkward fit, if not downright difficult and burdensome, for someone with his temperament and social background. The arts of ingratiation that Lincoln had learned and depended on were geared toward an exclusively male audience and were therefore useless. To make a suitable impression in this circle, a young man was expected to be formal and gracious complimentary and deferential, witty if possible, and tastefully flirtatious when the occasion allowed.[20]

MELANCHOLY

The social pressures and feelings of inadequacy undoubtedly increased Lincoln's

Abraham Lincoln and Bipolar Disorder

Bipolar disorder, another name for manic-depression, is a mental illness or biochemical brain disorder characterized by a pattern of mood swings. In the manic phase, the person feels extremely energetic and believes himself or herself to be especially creative, intelligent, and aware. There is often a period of hypomania (a mild mania) where the person feels especially positive and is often quite creative. Usually, after the manic energy is spent, the person becomes extremely depressed and may feel hopeless, anxious, irritable, even guilty, losing sight of all accomplishments. If severe, the person's thinking may become delusional or psychotic. Depression alternating with intense or psychotic manias is referred to as Bipolar I. Depression with only hypomania (no psychosis or loss of control) is referred to as Bipolar II. Generally, bipolar adults are able to live normally between the periods of extreme mood swings.

In Moodswing, Dr. Ronald R. Fieve, an expert in treating depression, writes, "Abraham Lincoln's recurrent states of despair and exhaustion, alternating with periods of hard work and very effective functioning, were what I would consider a mild form of bipolar manic-depression (now referred to as Bipolar II)."

The Substance Abuse and Mental Health Services Administration (SAMHSA), a division of the U.S. Department of Health and Human Services Administration, states:

From the time he was a teenager, Abraham Lincoln lived with what today some people think might have been depression and bipolar disorder. . . . Most Americans are aware that Abraham Lincoln held the country together throughout the Civil War. Many Americans, however, are unaware that through most of his adult life Abraham Lincoln was fighting yet another war—the war within himself.

anxiety and contributed to his mood swings and unrelenting bouts with depression. Though Lincoln had had periods of depression in New Salem, and he had suffered an emotional crisis after Ann Rutledge died, no one described him as sad or melancholy until he lived in Springfield. It was there that people began to notice and mention his melancholy and there that it became a conspicuous part of his personality and demeanor. William Henry Herndon, who later became his law partner and later still his biographer, described him as "a sad-looking man; his melancholy dripped from him as he walked."[21] This description of a man known, loved, and admired for his humor and good nature may seem incompatible with the Lincoln image. But that melancholy was also an integral, fundamental part of his being. There was a duality, and it also became apparent in Springfield. Wilson described that, as well, in *Honor's Voice*:

> From his arrival in Springfield in 1837, and possibly sometime before, Lincoln's divided nature began to make itself evident. His melancholy became more visible and presumably more pronounced, but he continued to be a conspicuous source of hilarity and conviviality among his acquaintances. Herndon told his collaborator that "Mr. L. had a double consciousness, a double life. . . . In one moment he was in a state of abstraction and then quickly in another state when he was a social, talkative, and a communicative fellow."[22]

FATALISM

After years of observation and contemplation, Herndon concluded that the source of Lincoln's melancholy was hereditary and part of his nature. (This was an astute conclusion, particularly for that time. Today, many experts believe that Lincoln's behavior would warrant a diagnosis of bipolar disorder.) Herndon connected this melancholia to Lincoln's sense of foreboding. Several times, according to Herndon, Lincoln told him ominously, "Billy, I feel as if I shall meet with some terrible end."[23] More than just a foreboding or premonition, this was in keeping with the fatalistic outlook that pervaded Lincoln's life. Although he was not a churchgoer, Lincoln had been raised in a Baptist household. He believed in the Doctrine of Necessity, which maintains that the actions of any individual are predetermined and shaped by the unknowable wishes of a Higher Power. He had always had the sense that his destiny was controlled by a Higher Power and that "perhaps he might be an instrument in God's hands of accomplishing a great work and he certainly was not unwilling to be."[24] This idea fed his ambition, making him strive to fulfill that destiny. But it set up a moral dilemma, for he also believed that individuals are responsible for their own acts, a position that could not be entirely reconciled with the fatalistic belief that what is to be will be.

Lincoln's mood swings were apparent in his ambition and confidence when he was "up" and in his gloomy assessments of his accomplishments when he was "down." And these moods were reflected in statements he made about wanting to be remembered for actions that benefited humankind, contrasted with his despairing that "he had done nothing to make any human being remember that he had lived."[25]

MARY TODD: A ROCKY BEGINNING

The tendency toward emotional extremes was also evident in Lincoln's anxieties

THE BEGINNING OF A FRIENDSHIP

Joshua Speed was Lincoln's closest friend. They lived together for four years and, as was common among young men in the nineteenth-century West, they even slept in the same bed. Quoted from "Reminiscences of Abraham Lincoln" in Lincoln: As I Knew Him, *Speed remembers his first impression of Lincoln and how their friendship began.*

It was in the spring of 1837, and on the very day that he obtained his [law] license, that our intimate acquaintance began. He had ridden into town on a borrowed horse, with no earthly property save a pair of saddle-bags containing a few clothes. I was a merchant at Springfield, and kept a large country store. . . . Lincoln came into the store with his saddle-bags on his arm. He said he wanted to buy the furniture for a single bed. The mattress, blankets, sheets, coverlid, and pillow, according to the figures made by me, would cost seventeen dollars. He said that was perhaps cheap enough; but, small as the sum was, he was unable to pay it. But if I would credit him till Christmas, and his experiment as a lawyer was a success, he would pay then, saying, in the saddest tone, "If I fail in this, I do not know that I can ever pay you." As I looked up at him I thought then, and think now, that I never saw a sadder face.

I said to him, "You seem to be so much pained at contracting so small a debt, I think I can suggest a plan by which you can avoid the debt and at the same time attain your end. I have a large room with a double bed upstairs, which you are very welcome to share with me." "Where is your room?" said he. "Upstairs," said I, pointing to a pair of winding stairs which led from the store to my room.

He took his saddle-bags on his arm, went upstairs, set them down on the floor, and came down with the most changed countenance. Beaming with pleasure he exclaimed, "Well, Speed, I am moved!" Mr. Lincoln was then twenty-seven years old—a lawyer without a client, no money, all his earthly wealth consisting of the clothes he wore and the contents of his saddle-bags.

about his relationships with women. When he met Mary Todd, a pretty and cultured young woman from a wealthy family, he was infatuated with her, as were many other young men. The couple became engaged, and soon after Lincoln, for reasons that remain a mystery, broke it off. (Some historians believe he was overwhelmed by his tempestuous emotions.) Then after the breakup, he became utterly despondent, staying locked in his room for a week, unable to sleep, and afterward

Lincoln was captivated by Mary Todd, and the couple married in 1842.

ABRAHAM AND MARY

Abraham and Mary Lincoln were opposites in many ways besides their background. He was tall and thin; she was short and slightly plump. He was unconcerned with—even unaware of—dress and appearance; she was quite vain. He was quick-witted and droll, known for his humor and compassion; she was vivacious and charming, though humorless, known for her temper tantrums and her frequently sharp tongue. He was moody and often withdrawn; she was lively, talkative, and outgoing. But they were fond of and devoted to one another. And they had things in common. They loved the same poetry, and enjoyed reciting it. Both had dark moods. They both had lost their mothers at an early age. Both loved politics and were devout Whigs. In fact Henry Clay, the leader of the Whig party, was a Todd family friend and frequent visitor to the Todd household when Mary was growing up.

And both Lincolns were very ambitious. Mary recognized her future husband's ambition, and recognized the traits and talents that would allow him to achieve greatness. She wanted to be part of it. Mary had once told her sister that she planned to be the wife of a president, and she later remarked, "He is to be president of the United States someday. If I had not thought so, I would never have married him, for you can see he is not pretty."[27]

After his marriage, Lincoln's mood swings between grandiosity (unrealistic overconfidence) and melancholia decreased somewhat, or at least were not so conspicuous. But Mary's horrible

appearing weak and emaciated. In a letter to Stuart, he wrote:

> I am now the most miserable man living. If what I feel were equally distributed to the whole human family, there would not be one cheerful face on earth. Whether I shall ever be better, I cannot tell; I awfully forbode I shall not. To remain as I am is impossible. I must die or be better, it appears to me.[26]

Finally, with help from friends Lincoln and Mary reunited, and in 1842 they were married in the parlor of her sister's home.

MARY TODD OR MATILDA EDWARDS?

After Lincoln ended his engagement to Mary Todd in January 1841, he sank into a depression so overwhelming that he was unable to attend the legislature for more than a week. Most historians have attributed Lincoln's breakdown to his despair over the breakup with Mary. In Honor's Voice, *Douglas L. Wilson has gathered evidence that supports a different story. According to several close friends of Lincoln, he fell deeply in love with a young woman named Matilda Edwards after he was engaged to Mary, and his despair resulted from his believing he had not lived up to his standard of honor, duty, and obligation toward his fiancée.*

When Mary first moved to Springfield in late 1839, she stayed with her sister and brother-in-law, Elizabeth and Ninian Edwards, and it was probably at one of their parties that she first met Lincoln. He was quite intrigued with Mary for she was bright, witty, and charming. Yet by all accounts, she was in pursuit of him. Because Lincoln was on the road campaigning, the couple was able to see each other only a few times. When Lincoln returned in November, he had lost interest in Mary and wanted to end the relationship, which had consisted mainly of correspondence.

Joshua Speed, Lincoln's close friend and confidant, told William Herndon that what caused Lincoln to fall out of love with Mary was another woman, Matilda Edwards. The account of Mary Todd's brother-in-law, Ninian W. Edwards, agrees with Speed's: He says that during Lincoln's courtship of Todd that he fell in love with [Edward's beautiful eighteen-year-old cousin] Matilda Edwards and the engagement was broken off.

Another account, that of James H. Matheny (best man at Lincoln's wedding), also supports this version. Wilson quotes Matheny as saying that "Lincoln often told him directly & indirectly that he was driven into the marriage— Said it was Concocted & planned by the Edwards family."

Wilson, in a detailed analysis of conversations, letters, events, and schedules, presents a well-documented case for the lesser-known version. He concludes that:

The conventional view of the courtship is not supported by contemporary documents, such as Mary's own letters and those of her friends; it pays no heed to what Lincoln's closest friend and confidant, Joshua Speed, said about the origin and timing of the affair; and it also ignores the clear and consistent testimony of those closest to the principals that Lincoln said at the time that he did not love Mary but loved Matilda Edwards instead.

headaches (which she attributed to allergies and were probably migraines) and outbursts of temper increased. Once, when Lincoln was absorbed in reading and Mary was angry because she thought he was ignoring her, she hit him on the nose with a piece of firewood.

PRACTICING LAW

As Lincoln had promised with his reelection in 1840, he did not run for Congress again in 1842. And he lost the Whig nomination for his old seat in 1843, but that did not diminish his desire or ambition. For the time being, he was satisfied with his selection as a Whig elector for the 1844 presidential race.

Finances were tight for Lincoln, who was trying to support his wife and infant son Robert Todd, born on August 1, 1843, and to pay for the only home the Lincolns ever owned. He worked hard building his law practice, and he traveled with the judge of the circuit court twice a year for about ten weeks (as did many of the Springfield attorneys) to serve as counsel for litigants. Because he could not earn enough money to support his family by practicing only in Springfield, circuit riding became necessary as another source of income. It helped Lincoln politically later because his reputation for integrity and fairness grew, and he met many attorneys and clients who became his supporters.

Although Lincoln had continually practiced law since moving to Springfield, he changed partners several times. In 1841, Lincoln ended his association with

Stuart and became the partner of Stephen Logan. In 1844, he ended his partnership with Logan and started his own practice with junior partner Herndon, who remained a close friend all his life.

CONGRESS AND WASHINGTON, D.C.

In 1846 Lincoln was nominated for Congress by the Whigs. He ran a successful campaign and won the election, but the session did not begin until December 6, 1847, leaving plenty of time to prepare for the move to Washington, D.C. Meanwhile, on March 10, 1846, his second son, Edward Baker, was born, making the Lincolns' small house even more crowded, and putting additional strain on Mary. Having been raised in luxury with slaves, Mrs. Lincoln was ill prepared to do housework and child care at all, much less by herself.

When the Lincolns first moved to Washington, D.C., it was new and exciting and a welcome escape for Mary. The young couple quickly came to enjoy the cultural advantages and intellectual stimulation of a large city. But soon Lincoln became busier with commitments and the newness wore off. The capital lost its appeal for Mary who took the children back to Kentucky, where they stayed with her father. Lincoln was left by himself and greatly missed Mary and the boys. He also arrived at a hardening of a lifelong moral stand. For two thousand of the forty thousand residents of the District of Columbia were slaves, and he now saw how slaves lived and were treated under this system. This firsthand look at the horrors of slavery led

Lincoln's home in Springfield, Illinois, after the second story was added.

Lincoln, who had always opposed it on moral and philosophical grounds, to realize that the institution was the antithesis of everything the United States was supposed to stand for, and that his beloved country could never truly be the land of liberty as long as slavery existed.

DISENCHANTMENT WITH WHIGS

Lincoln worked hard for the election of the Whig candidate for president, Zachary Taylor, hoping the party would unite behind the principles he had believed it represented. During his only term in Congress, he attempted to introduce only one bill, which proposed a referendum on slavery in the District of Columbia and compensation to any slave owners who freed their slaves. But it was a compromise, designed to end the debates that were threatening his party, and it was opposed by both antislavery and proslavery forces, so he never introduced it. After having worked so hard for the Whigs to help Taylor become president, Lincoln believed he deserved a political reward—the appointment he sought as commissioner of the General Land Office. He was terribly disappointed when he did not get it and refused the appointment he was offered instead, the governorship of the Oregon Territory. Lincoln was becoming increasingly disenchanted with the Whigs, particularly in the party's inability to arrive at a clear, morally acceptable position on the slavery issue.

4 A Roundabout Route to the Presidency

After leaving Congress, Lincoln devoted himself to his legal career, assuming his career in politics was over. He moved his family back to Springfield, where he had more time for reflection and self-improvement. Because he believed his program of self-education was inadequate and that he lacked discipline, Lincoln decided to study Euclid's principles of geometry in an attempt to exercise and sharpen his mental faculties, especially his powers of logic and language. He eventually mastered the first six books of Euclid. Thus fortified, he was ready to return to legal work.

It was easy for Lincoln to reestablish his practice once he returned to Springfield. Many old clients remained or returned, and new ones were attracted by his record and reputation. Lincoln shared duties with his partner, William Herndon. Herndon, a voracious reader and a thorough man, did the research. Lincoln did the

Springfield, Illinois, in 1869. The law offices of Lincoln and his partner, William Herndon, are located in the second-to-last building at the end of the block.

paperwork and appeared in court. As a team, they developed a thriving practice before the Illinois Supreme Court and the circuit and district courts in Illinois.

CIRCUIT COURT

During the late 1840s and early 1850s, the majority of Lincoln's law practice was in the circuit courts. Thus he traveled from county to county representing litigants in matters that were primarily of interest and significance only to the parties involved, but he was performing an essential service. Circuit riding was a nomadic existence, with poor accommodations on the circuit, but given Lincoln's characteristic indifference to his surroundings and personal comfort, the lack of amenities did not bother him. Henry Clay Whitney, an attorney who rode the eighth judicial circuit with Lincoln, gave a vivid description of the circuit:

> At the tavern the lawyers slept two in a bed and three or four beds were located in one room: at meals, the Judge, lawyers, suitors, jurors, witnesses Court officers, and prisoners out on bail all ate together and carried on in a running conversation all along the line of a long dining room.

> When one Court was through, the Judge and lawyers would tumble into a farmer's wagon, or a carryall, or a succession of buggies, and trundle off across the prairie to another court, stopping by the way at a farm house for a chance dinner.

In this kind of unsteady, nomadic life, Lincoln passed about four months each year; he had no clerk, no stenographer, no library, no method or system of business, but carried his papers in his hat or coat pocket. The consideration and trial of each case began and ended with itself, he was continually roused to devise a new policy—new tactics—fresh expedients, with each new retainer.[28]

Lincoln traveled basically the same circuit, an area approximately the size of Connecticut, twice a year. He was always in demand, and his skill and his reputation steadily grew. Even though he was only forty, he was one of the senior lawyers on the circuit, and the younger attorneys relied on him for assistance. It was during this period that he became known as "Honest Abe," because he was admired for his honesty, fairness, and devotion to hard work and detail.

And he was admired for his extraordinary skill and performance in the courtroom. Often initially underestimated because of his appearance and manner, opponents soon learned they had been outwitted and defeated by a master. John H. Littlefield, who studied law in the Lincoln-Herndon office, wrote his recollection of Lincoln in an article published in *The Independent* in 1895:

> As a lawyer, in his opening speech before the jury, he would cut all the "dead wood" out of the case. The client would sometimes become alarmed, thinking that Lincoln had given away so much of the case that he would not

have anything left. After he had shuffled off the necessary surplusage he would get down to "hard pan," and state the case so clearly that it would soon be apparent he had enough left to win the case with. In making such concessions he would so establish his position in fairness and honesty that the lawyer on the opposite side would scarcely have the heart to oppose what he contended for.[29]

Lincoln was also a clever cross-examiner and a master of legal tactics. He closed his cases with clear, logical arguments that were bold and energetic. A good example, and probably his most famous criminal case, was the trial of William "Duff" Armstrong for the murder of James Metzker, where a witness claimed that by the light of the moon overhead he clearly saw Armstrong attack Metzker. After skillfully questioning the witness, making him retell his story several times, Lincoln destroyed the man's testimony by producing an almanac that proved the moon had already set at the time the witness claimed it had illuminated the attack. As usual, he won the case.

THE HOME FRONT

At home, things were not going as well. In December 1849, Edward, almost four, became gravely ill. On February 1, 1850, after a long bout with pulmonary tuberculosis, he died, devastating both parents. Always an unstable person, Mary moved a little closer to the edge, foreshadowing

her ultimate breakdown. A few weeks after Eddie's death, Mary was pregnant again, and William Wallace "Willie" was born on December 21, 1850; Thomas, named after Lincoln's father, and nicknamed Tad because his unusually large head and small body reminded Lincoln of a tadpole, was born April 4, 1853. After the death of Eddie, Lincoln paid increasingly more attention to his two small children, becoming quite indulgent and in effect allowing them free rein. When Mary was unable to care for them, either because she was overwhelmed or was having one of her tantrums, he would baby-sit. Lincoln welcomed these times in the company of his young sons, for he had been unable to spend time with Robert, his oldest boy, when he was growing up, and he did not want to miss the opportunity to be close to Willie and Tad. At that time, however, childcare by fathers was almost unheard of, and Lincoln's performance of these duties was considered to be very unusual. Contemporary critics said that he was henpecked.

Meanwhile, Mary's behavior became progressively more erratic, probably intensified by the strain of Eddie's death followed by the two births. At times she was cheerful and engaging, functioning with kindness and generosity among family members and in the community. But at times, for no apparent reason, she would explode, particularly at her husband. One time, according to a neighbor, she chased him out of the house and down the street with a butcher knife. She was also fearful and anxious, terrified of things such as thunderstorms, burglars, and dogs. And

William Herndon was Lincoln's law partner, friend, and later biographer. Because of his close association with Lincoln, he was able to provide personal observations and insights such as these quoted in *Lincoln: As I Knew Him*:

Morning Routine

In the office, as in the court room, Lincoln, when discussing any point, was never arbitrary or insinuating. He was deferential, cool, patient, and respectful. When he reached the office, about nine o'clock in the morning, the first thing he did was to pick up a newspaper, spread himself out on an old sofa, one leg on a chair, and read aloud, much to my discomfort. Singularly enough Lincoln never read any other way but aloud. This habit used to annoy me almost beyond the point of endurance. I once asked him why he did so. This was his explanation: "When I read aloud two senses catch the idea; first, I see what I read; second, I hear it, and therefore I can remember it better."

Melancholia Routine

Mr. Lincoln never had a confidant, and therefore never unbosomed himself to others. He never spoke of his trials to me or, so far as I knew, to any of his friends. It was a great burden to carry, but he bore it sadly enough and without a murmur. I could always realize when he was in distress, without being told. He was not exactly an early riser, that is, he never usually appeared in the office till about nine o'clock in the morning. I usually preceded him an hour. Sometimes, however, he would come down as early as seven o'clock—in fact on one occasion I remember he came down before daylight. If, on arriving at the office, I found him in, I knew instantly that a breeze had sprung up over the domestic sea, and that the waters were troubled. He would either be lying on the lounge looking skyward, or doubled up in a chair with his feet resting on the sill of a back window. He would not look up on my entering, and only answered my "Good morning" with a grunt. I at once busied myself with pen and paper, or ran through the leaves of some books; but the evidence of his melancholy and distress was so plain, and his silence so significant, that I would grow restless myself, and finding some excuse to go [to] the court house or elsewhere, would leave the room.

The Lincolns' young sons Tad (left) and Willie in 1861. Their mother's erratic behavior caused Lincoln to indulge his sons.

she suffered from migraine headaches that sent her to bed for days at a time. She needed an increasing amount of assistance and reassurance from her husband, who himself was prone to periods of depression and mental anguish.

THE SLAVERY ISSUE LEADS TO REENTRY INTO POLITICS

About the same time Lincoln was attempting to cope with the loss of his son Eddie, Congress was struggling with the slavery issue. It was tearing the country apart, and in an attempt to prevent the Southern states from seceding, Congress passed five acts, which together were known as the Compromise of 1850. And Lincoln, who opposed the extension of slavery into new territories, supported the compromise: He hoped that its concessions to both the pro- and antislavery factions would preserve the Union. Historians generally agree, however, that the measures merely delayed the Civil War ten years.

In 1854 an earlier set of slavery-related laws called the Missouri Compromise was repealed by the passage of the Kansas-Nebraska Act, which also allowed settlers to decide by popular vote whether slavery would be allowed in the territories of Kansas and Nebraska. It was then that Lincoln reentered the political arena as a candidate for the U.S. Senate. He had been unhappy and frustrated while not holding political office, but the repeal of the Missouri Compromise, as he once said, "aroused him as he had never been before."[30] He began to speak out against the Kansas-Nebraska Act eloquently and vehemently, particularly with respect to the issue of slavery.

Lincoln's opponent in the election, incumbent Illinois senator Stephen Douglas, had authored the act and with it the concept of "popular sovereignty," which meant the residents of new territories (here, Kansas and Nebraska) would be able to decide for themselves whether to allow slavery. Lincoln was opposed to popular sovereignty because it allowed the first settlers to decide the question of slavery for all who would later live there, robbing these later residents of their voice in the democratic process. He was also afraid it would create competition between Northerners and Southerners wanting to settle the land. And fundamentally, he believed that the Kansas-Nebraska Act, far from confirming that slavery was dying out, as some proponents claimed, proved that supporters of the intolerable institution were gaining influence.

LINCOLN CHALLENGES DOUGLAS

Lincoln tried to get Douglas to debate him, but Douglas refused. So on October 3, 1854, after Douglas spoke in the hall of the House of Representatives to defend the Kansas-Nebraska Act, as the audience was leaving Lincoln announced from the stairway that he would answer Douglas

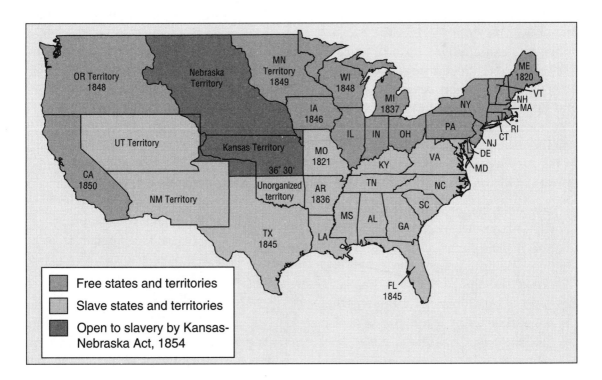

THE KANSAS-NEBRASKA ACT

Senator Stephen A. Douglas introduced the Kansas-Nebraska Act into Congress, and it was passed in 1854. It provided for the establishment of two new U.S. territories, Kansas and Nebraska, from the Indian land that was north of 37 degrees latitude and west of the bend of the Missouri River.

To win the support of Southern congressmen, Douglas included a provision for popular sovereignty, which stated that all questions of slavery in the new territories would be decided by the settlers rather than by Congress. The Kansas-Nebraska Act repealed the Missouri Compromise of 1820 (which had declared that all land in the Louisiana Purchase north of 36 degrees 30 minutes, except Missouri, would be free and maintained the balance between free and slave states) and produced a violent reaction from Americans who were opposed to slavery.

The Kansas-Nebraska Act was especially significant because it made slavery legal in a vast new area, reviving the clash over the expansion of slavery, and it accelerated the start of the Civil War. On a personal level, it compelled Lincoln to reenter the political arena.

the next day and offered him a chance to respond. The following day, Lincoln spoke to a large crowd in the House of Representatives hall for three hours. Most of his arguments had been made before and appealed to reason. But he became emotional when he pointed out that whether residents of a state were entitled to permit slavery depended on whether or not blacks were men:

> The doctrine of self-government is right—absolutely and eternally right—but it has no just application, as here attempted. Or perhaps I should rather say that whether it has such application depends upon whether a negro is *not* or *is* a man. . . . But if the negro *is* a man, is it not to that extent a total destruction of self-government, to say that he too shall not govern *himself*? When the white man governs himself that is self-government. But when he governs himself, and also governs *another* man, that is *more* than self-government—that is despotism. If the negro is a *man*, why then my ancient faith teaches me that "all men are created equal"; and that there can be no moral right in connection with one man's making a slave of another. . . . What I do say is, that no man is good enough to govern another man, *without that other's consent*. I say this is the leading principle—the sheet anchor of American republicanism.[31]

And that was, he maintained, where he differed from Douglas, because Douglas had "no very vivid impression that the negro is a human; and consequently has no idea that there can be any moral question in legislating about him."[32] It was an eloquent and emotional speech. Douglas responded with a rebuttal that was almost two hours long.

FAVORING DEPORTATION

Lincoln's attitude toward slavery derived from the Declaration of Independence, with its core assumption that "all men are created equal." Slavery, then, violated the American ideals of equality and liberty. And he had been trying to figure a way to deal with the problems caused by slavery in America. In 1854, colonization (the term used at the time for deporting and resettling blacks in Africa) seemed the answer to him. Lincoln wanted to relocate all freed slaves to Liberia, a small independent state in West Africa that had begun as a colony of freedmen governed by white Americans. He thought that would solve several problems. It would remove the people many white Southerners regarded as troublemakers—free blacks who were literate and, it was feared, capable of effectively organizing unhappy slaves. And slave owners would be more likely to free their slaves if they knew they would be shipped to Africa instead of remaining near the plantations to be disruptive. Also, Northerners would be more supportive of emancipation if the freedmen were shipped to Africa, rather than migrating to free states and competing with white laborers. Lincoln thought

voluntary emigration would do well "in freeing our land from the dangerous presence of slavery" and "in restoring a captive people to their long-lost fatherland, with bright prospects for the future."[33]

It sounded logical, but in reality, was not feasible. The freedmen had been born and raised in the United States and most did not want to go to Africa. Slave owners would not willingly free their slaves, whom they regarded as property they had paid for, and Northerners would not pay to transport and settle the emigrants in Africa.

REPUBLICANS

Lincoln dedicated himself to opposing the spread of slavery, which he argued "was a great moral evil, fundamentally incompatible with democracy."[34] He spoke with passion, logic, and a new tone—moral outrage. He had found his voice and his purpose. And he was rewarded with the offer of a seat in the state legislature, which he declined in favor of seeking the Senate seat. Lincoln would have been ineligible to run for the Senate as a member of the Illinois legislature because at that time, U.S. senators were chosen by their respective state legislatures.

Lincoln narrowly lost election to the Senate in 1855 and was terribly disappointed. He felt betrayed by his party, especially after all he had put into it, and blamed his defeat on political backstabbing. He became increasingly disillusioned with the Whigs and was drawn to the new Republican Party, which was committed to stopping the spread of slavery. It grew out of a coalition of abolitionist Whigs and Democrats who opposed the Kansas-Nebraska Act.

At the first Republican Convention in May of 1856, Lincoln gave the final major speech before adjourning, a speech that has often been called his best speech. But there is no copy or record of that speech, which Lincoln apparently made on the spur of the moment, without a prepared text. According to highlights in a local paper, Lincoln said he was "ready to fuse with anyone who would unite with him to oppose slave power," and urged all who opposed the expansion of slavery to unite. Further he said, "The Union must be preserved in the purity of its principles as well as in the integrity of its territorial parts,"[35] foreshadowing what would become his ultimate goal.

Herndon also attended, and though he initially attempted to take notes of Lincoln's speech, as he always did when Lincoln spoke in public, he stopped after about fifteen minutes and "lived only in the inspiration of the hour."[36] He later recalled, "His speech was full of fire and energy and force; it was logic; it was pathos; it was enthusiasm; it was justice, equity, truth, and right set ablaze by the divine fires of a soul maddened by the wrong; it was hard, heavy, knotty, gnarly, backed with wrath."[37] Lincoln received 110 votes for vice president and though he believed that he was making progress politically, he temporarily removed himself from politics so that he could take care of his private affairs.

LINCOLN-DOUGLAS DEBATES

The year 1857 was the busiest and most successful one ever for the Lincoln and Herndon law firm. And much to Mary's delight, a second story was added to the Lincoln's small house. A Supreme Court decision in March of that year ultimately compelled Lincoln to come forward and challenge his old political rival, Stephen Douglas. Dred Scott was a slave who moved with his master from Missouri, a slave state, to Illinois, a free state, and then to the Wisconsin territory, also free. Scott lived on free soil for many years before returning with his master to Mis-

Lincoln was incensed by judicial treatment of Dred Scott. According to the Supreme Court, civil liberties did not extend to blacks.

FIFTH LINCOLN-DOUGLAS DEBATE

The fifth debate, at Knox College in Galesburg, Illinois, on October 7, 1858, drew fifteen thousand, the largest crowd of the seven debates. Lincoln aggressively responded to Douglas's contention that the authors of the Declaration of Independence meant only "white men . . . of European birth, and European descent." This excerpt is from Lincoln on Democracy, *edited by Mario M. Cuomo:*

The Judge [Douglas] has alluded to the Declaration of Independence, and insisted that negroes are not included in that Declaration; and that it is a slander upon the framers of that instrument, to suppose that negroes were meant therein; and he asks you: Is it possible to believe that Mr. Jefferson, who penned the immortal paper, could have supposed himself applying the language of that instrument to the negro race, and yet held a portion of that race in slavery? Would he not at once have freed them? I only have to remark upon this part of the Judge's speech, (and that, too, very briefly, for I shall not detain myself, or you, upon that point for any great length of time,) that I believe the entire records of the world, from the date of the Declaration of Independence up to within three years ago, may be searched in vain for one single affirmation, from one single man, that the negro was not included in the Declaration of Independence. I think I may defy Judge Douglas to show that he [Jefferson] ever said so, that Washington ever said so, that any President ever said so, that any member of Congress ever said so, or that any living man upon the whole earth ever said so until the necessities of the present policy of the Democratic party, in regard to slavery, had to invent that affirmation. [Tremendous applause.]

souri. When his master died in Missouri, Scott attempted to sue for his freedom because he had previously lived in a free state. The Supreme Court ruled that no slave or descendant of a slave could be a citizen of the United States, and as a noncitizen Scott did not have the right to sue and must remain a slave. What disturbed Lincoln was the Court's claim that the Declaration of Independence and the Constitution did not intend to include blacks. He was outraged and vowed to see the decision overturned.

In 1858, Lincoln easily won the nomination for senator of the new Republican Party and accepted it with his famous House Divided speech. He and the incumbent Stephen Douglas delivered many speeches (Douglas 130 and Lincoln 63) before they met face-to-face. Then they finally agreed to a series of seven now-legendary debates that were the highlight

Lincoln speaks at one of his famous debates with Stephen Douglas during the 1858 senatorial campaign in Illinois.

of the 1858 campaign. Wherever they met, there were bands, parades, fireworks, and cannons. Interest was high, and the candidates debated before enthusiastic crowds that often reached fifteen thousand. Although both men were eloquent, powerful, persuasive orators, in every other way they were as different as their political positions. Lincoln was tall, gangly, humbly dressed, and unpretentious. Douglas, known as "The Little Giant," was short, stocky, stylishly dressed, and sophisticated. Lincoln traveled in a regular pas-

senger train; Douglas had a private railroad car. Lincoln appeared awkward and spoke in a high, piercing voice, while Douglas was poised and had a low, booming voice.

Douglas argued for popular sovereignty, declaring he did not care whether slavery was voted up or down, only that the decision be made by a majority vote of the residents. He also tried to portray Lincoln as an extreme abolitionist who would free slaves to take jobs away from white men and to marry their daughters.

Douglas believed that blacks were inferior and that the country was founded to be governed by whites for whites.

Lincoln, somewhat on the defensive, explained he did not believe in interracial marriage or blacks' right to vote. Despite his abhorrence of slavery, Lincoln lived and ran for office in a racist society. For the time, his views were far from mainstream; he would never be elected if he appeared too extreme. And at that time he did believe there was a difference be-tween the races that would make total social and political equality impossible. Lincoln was emphatic, however, that the Declaration of Independence applied to blacks and that they must be given the right to liberty and equality of opportunity.

In the seventh and final debate, Lincoln eloquently brought the issue back to fundamentals—right and wrong:

> He [Douglas] says that upon the score of equality, slaves should be allowed

THE HOUSE DIVIDED SPEECH, SPRINGFIELD, ILLINOIS, JUNE 16, 1858

Having been nominated for the U.S. Senate, Lincoln closed the Republican convention and launched his campaign with this famous speech. At the time, some of his supporters felt it was too radical. The opening remarks are reprinted from Abraham Lincoln: His Speeches and Writings:

If we could first know *where* we are, and *whither* we are tending, we could the better judge *what* to do, and *how* to do it.

We are now far into the *fifth* year, since a policy was initiated, with the *avowed* object, and *confident* promise, of putting an end to slavery agitation.

Under the operation of that policy, that agitation has not only, not *ceased*, but has *constantly augmented.*

In my opinion, it *will* not cease, until a *crisis* shall have been reached, and passed—"A house divided against itself cannot stand."

I believe this government cannot endure, permanently half *slave* and half *free.*

I do not expect the Union to be *dissolved*—I do not expect the house to *fall*—but I *do* expect it will cease to be divided.

It will become *all* one thing, or *all* the other.

Either the *opponents* of slavery, will arrest the further spread of it, and place it where the public mind shall rest in the belief that it is in course of ultimate extinction; or its *advocates* will push it forward, till it shall become alike lawful in *all* the States, *old* as well as *new*—*North* as well as *South.* . . .

to go in a new Territory, like other property. This is strictly logical if there is no difference between it and other property. If it and other property are equal, his argument is entirely logical. But if you insist that one is wrong and the other is right, there is no use to institute a comparison between right and wrong. . . .

That is the real issue. That is the issue that will continue in this country when these poor tongues of Judge Douglas and myself shall be silent. It is the eternal struggle between these two principles that have stood face to face from the beginning of time, and will ever continue to struggle. The one is the common right of humanity and the other the divine right of kings. It is the same principle in whatever shape it develops itself. It is the same spirit that says, "You work and toil and earn bread, and I'll eat it."[38]

LINCOLN WINS PRESIDENCY

Because senators were chosen by state legislators rather than by popular vote, as has been done since the passage of the Seventeenth Amendment in 1913, and because the legislature was Democratic, Douglas won the vote. Lincoln was, once again, terribly disappointed to have lost,

but still it was not a rejection by the voters. In any event, he had gained exposure and stature through the debates and had acquired a national following. As a leader of the Republican Party, he was seen as a future candidate for president, especially since he held the middle ground between the two extremes—the abolitionists and the slaveholders.

Lincoln started preparing to run for the presidency by giving political speeches in Ohio, Wisconsin, Iowa, and Kansas Territory and seeking a publisher for his transcripts of the debates, which were published in 1860 with an introduction he wrote. In New York, despite initial misgivings about his gawky and countrified appearance, he gave a speech that roused the sophisticated audience and established him as a serious and capable politician.

Although he chose not to attend the Republican National Convention, Lincoln won the nomination on the third ballot, and Maine Senator Hannibal Hamlin was nominated for vice president. Assisted by the Democrats splitting—with the Northern faction nominating Senator Douglas and the Southern faction nominating John Breckinridge—and the Constitutional Union Party offering a fourth candidate, John Bell, Lincoln won the election with 40 percent of the popular vote and 180 electoral votes. The other three candidates received a combined total of 123 electoral votes.

5 For the Union

Election Day on November 6, 1860, had one of the largest voter turnouts in U.S. history: 81 percent of the eligible voters went to the polls. Much was at stake. The country was divided over slavery, and the winner of the election would determine national policy on that issue. With the victory of Abraham Lincoln, the candidate most hostile to slavery, Southerners believed that both their economy and their way of life were in jeopardy. Lincoln had repeatedly reassured the South that his goal was to preserve the Union, not to abolish slavery, and that he would not interfere with slavery in the states where it already existed, but the Southern states were still antagonistic. Lincoln had won the election, but the country was still divided, and prospects for a successful administration were far from good. The possibility that Southern states would secede, or withdraw from the Union, loomed ever larger.

SECESSION

On December 20, 1860, two and a half months before Lincoln was to be inaugurated, South Carolina seceded. There had been threats of secession for years, but by the end of January, Florida, Mississippi, Alabama, Georgia, and Louisiana had followed South Carolina out of the Union, seizing federal arsenals and forts within their borders. February saw the formation of a rebel government, called the Confederate States of America, with Jefferson Davis as its president.

Southerners, now called Confederates, were extremely bitter and angry, and their hatred and rage were directed at Lincoln personally. He received hate mail and death threats, and an assassination plot was uncovered while he was on the train en route to Washington, D.C., for his inauguration.

Still, Lincoln believed most Southerners were patriots and reasonable people, but he rejected all contentions that secession was a legitimate public policy option. In a conversation with his secretary John G. Nicolay soon after his election, Lincoln made his commitment clear:

> The right of a state to secede is not an open or debatable question. It is the duty of a president to execute the laws and maintain the existing Government. He cannot entertain any

In 1860, seven Southern states seceded from the Union, forming the Confederate States of America. Jefferson Davis (pictured) became president of the rebel government.

proposition for dissolution or dismemberment. . . . No state can, in any way lawfully, get out of the Union, without the consent of the others.[39]

THE CIVIL WAR BEGINS

Lincoln had promised in his inaugural address, "The government will not assail you. You can have no conflict, without yourselves the aggressors."[40] So in April 1861, when a naval expedition carrying supplies and reinforcements to Fort Sumter,

South Carolina, was fired on and forced to retreat, Lincoln hesitated—and agonized. The Confederates had not seized the fort from the Union soldiers manning it, and Lincoln, while determined to keep Sumter under Union control was determined, also, not to initiate hostilities. And he truly hoped the Southerners would relent. Finally, he notified the governor of South Carolina that he was sending in provisions and if there was no resistance, he would not send in troops, arms, or ammunition. Lincoln knew this veiled ultimatum would create a crisis in the new Confederate command, for he had cleverly left the decision to fire with Jefferson Davis. Davis made that decision. On April 12, 1861, at 4:30 A.M., the shelling started. After thirty-three hours, Union soldiers surrendered, and the Rebel flag was flown over the fort. The Civil War had begun.

On April 15, Lincoln officially declared a rebellion was in progress and called seventy-five thousand volunteers into service for a period of ninety days; on April 19, he ordered a blockade of Southern ports. He was still convinced that the majority of Southerners were Unionists and that one solid victory would end the rebellion and solve the problem. He underestimated the depth of the secessionists' feelings, their dedication, and the dramatic difference between their views and goals and those of the Union.

INAUGURAL REMINDER

In his inaugural address, Lincoln had eloquently attempted to reassure, unify,

FAREWELL ADDRESS AT SPRINGFIELD, ILLINOIS
FEBRUARY 11, 1861

When Lincoln left for Washington to be inaugurated as the sixteenth president of the United States, he made an emotional farewell from the back of the train. This version, written aboard the train and found in Abraham Lincoln: His Speeches and Writings, *reveals not only his feelings about his neighbors and time spent in Springfield but also his acceptance of the monumental task before him:*

My friends—No one, not in my situation, can appreciate my feeling of sadness at this parting. To this place, and the kindness of these people, I owe everything. Here I have lived a quarter of a century, and have passed from a young to an old man. Here my children have been born, and one is buried. I now leave, not knowing when, or whether ever, I may return, with a task before me greater than that which rested upon Washington. Without the assistance of that Divine Being, who ever attended him [Washington], I cannot succeed. With that assistance I cannot fail. Trusting in Him, who can go with me, and remain with you, and be everywhere for good, let us confidently hope that all will yet be well. To His care commending you, as I hope in your prayers you will commend me, I bid you an affectionate farewell.

and warn, trying to avoid a civil war and to save the Union that some states believed they had already left forever. He began by quoting from previous speeches to remind the South that preserving the Union, not abolishing slavery, was his goal: "I have no purpose, directly or indirectly, to interfere with the institution of slavery in the States where it exists. I believe I have no lawful right to do so, and I have no inclination to do so."[41]

Later in the address, Lincoln explained why the Union was important. Although he refused to acknowledge the declarations of secession of six states, he spoke of the Union as perpetual, or unbreakable:

I hold, that in contemplation of universal law, and of the Constitution, The Union of these States is perpetual. Perpetuity is implied, if not expressed, in the fundamental law of all national governments. It is safe to assert that no government proper, ever had a provision in its organic law for its own termination. Continue to execute all the express provisions of our national Constitution, and the Union will endure forever—it being impossible to destroy it, except by some action not provided for in the instrument itself.

Descending from these general principles, we find the proposition

Lincoln's 1861 inauguration took place during the turbulent times preceding the Civil War.

that, in legal contemplation, the Union is perpetual, confirmed by the history of the Union itself. The Union is much older than the Constitution. It was formed in fact, by the Articles of Association in 1774. It was matured and continued by the Declaration of Independence in 1776. It was further matured and the faith of all the then thirteen States expressly plighted and engaged that it should be perpetual, by the Articles of Confederation in 1778. And finally, in 1787, one of the declared objects for ordaining and establishing the Constitution, was *"to form a more perfect union."*[42]

He ended, reluctantly—almost as if by continuing to talk, he could keep the country together and hold off the inevitable—by reminding North and South of shared history and bonds:

I am loth to close. We are not enemies, but friends. We must not be enemies.

Though passion may have strained, it must not break our bonds of affection. The mystic chords of memory, stretching from every battlefield, and patriot grave, to every living heart and hearthstone, all over this broad land, will yet swell the chorus of the Union, when again touched, as surely they will be, by the better angels of our nature.[43]

Abraham Lincoln revered the Union because it was derived from the Declaration of Independence, which recognized that all men are created equal and have the right to life, liberty, and the pursuit of happiness. The Union—the American experiment in democracy—was built on and embodied these truths, and it guaranteed everyone the same opportunity to pursue advancement that he had enjoyed. Lincoln could not allow the fundamental rights of Americans to slip away. He would do everything he could to preserve the Union.

SUSPENDING THE WRITANG OF *HABEAS CORPUS*

Saving the Union—which meant winning the war—was Lincoln's goal and he was determined to do whatever was necessary to accomplish it. Any temporary measures that were helpful, no matter how unprecedented or extreme, were undertaken without worrying about their constitutionality or long-term effects. One of the most criticized and controversial measures was the suspension of the privilege of the writ of *habeas corpus*. A writ of *habeas corpus* (literally meaning, "you should have the body") is an order from a judge to bring a prisoner before the court, where the legality of the person's imprisonment can be evaluated. The legal machinery whereby prisoners can demand to be informed of the charges against them so that a judge can rule on the legality of those charges has been a fundamental civil liberty of Americans since colonial times.

The suspension of the privilege of the writ of *habeas corpus* was unprecedented, but President Lincoln was convinced it was necessary to protect the capital, which was located between Maryland and Virginia, the most important of the upper Southern states. Virginia had already seceded and Maryland threatened to follow. And when secessionists blocked federal troops that were passing through Baltimore on the way to reinforce the capital, riots ensued. Bridges and telegraph lines into the city were destroyed, cutting Washington, D.C., off from the rest of the North. To make matters worse, there was a local militia organized to fight for the Confederacy, and there were rumors that the legislature was going to arm the state to fight against the Union. If Maryland seceded, Washington, D.C., would be permanently isolated. So Lincoln suspended the writ of *habeas corpus* from Washington to New York, and military officers were authorized to arrest anyone suspected of aiding the Confederacy. Because such prisoners could not petition for a writ of *habeas corpus* and were held by the

SPEECH IN INDEPENDENCE HALL, PHILADELPHIA, PENNSYLVANIA FEBRUARY 22, 1861

On his inaugural journey, Lincoln was inspired by a visit to Independence Hall to write this moving speech, which eloquently expresses his profound feelings about the Declaration of Independence. It was printed the next day in the Philadelphia Inquirer *and is reprinted in* Lincoln On Democracy.

I am filled with deep emotion at finding myself standing here in the place where were collected together the wisdom, the patriotism, the devotion to principle, from which sprang the institution under which we live. . . . I have never had a feeling politically that did not spring from the sentiments embodied in the Declaration of Independence. [Great cheering.] I have often pondered over the dangers which were incurred by the men who assembled here and adopted that Declaration of Independence—I have pondered over the toils that were endured by the officers and soldiers of the army, who achieved that Independence. [Applause] I have often inquired of myself, what great principle or idea it was that kept this Confederacy so long together. It was not the mere matter of the separation of the colonies from the mother land; but something in that Declaration giving liberty, not alone to the people of this country, but hope to the world for all future time. [Great applause.] It was that which gave promise that in due time the weights should be lifted from the shoulders of all men, and that *all* should have an equal chance. [Cheers.] This is the sentiment embodied in that Declaration of Independence. . . .

Now, in my view of the present aspect of affairs, there is no need of bloodshed and war. There is no necessity for it. I am not in favor of such a course, and I may say in advance, there will be no blood shed unless it be forced upon the Government. The Government will not use force unless force is used against it. [Prolonged applause and cries of "That's the proper sentiment."]

military, they could be detained indefinitely without a hearing and tried by a military tribunal.

In May when military officers arrested John Merryman, a prominent secessionist, his attorney petitioned for a writ of *habeas corpus*, but on Lincoln's instructions, the writ was not accepted. Chief Justice Roger B. Taney, a proslavery Democrat, then declared that Lincoln had acted unlawfully and that Congress, not the president, held the power of suspension.

Lincoln, of course, did not agree and ignored Taney. In his oath of office, he had sworn to "preserve, protect and defend the Constitution of the United States," which is what he believed he was doing. While the Constitution says, "The privilege of the writ of *habeas corpus* shall not be suspended," Article I, Section 9, adds "unless in cases of rebellion or invasion the public safety may require it." Even though Article I deals largely with the Congress, Section 9 does not say where the power to suspend *habeas corpus* lies. Lincoln seized the unattributed power. He believed that "the president could define the meaning of the Constitution and that the people themselves, in electing the president, also made constitutional law."[44]

Lincoln called an emergency session of Congress for July 4, two and a half months away, to defend his position. Almost one-third of his address to the reassembled Congress was a constitutional argument, answering Taney's charges that he had violated his oath that "the laws be faithfully executed" and that he had acted unconstitutionally. And he was convincing. The professor of constitutional law at Harvard, the leading constitutional lawyer in Congress, leaders of the American bar, and other prominent legal authorities supported him.

From the start, Lincoln had interpreted the Constitution in ways that increased presidential power. In *The Presidency of Abraham Lincoln*, historian Phillip Shaw Paludan explained:

> Thus the opening days of the Civil War brought a new and unprecedented strength to the presidency,

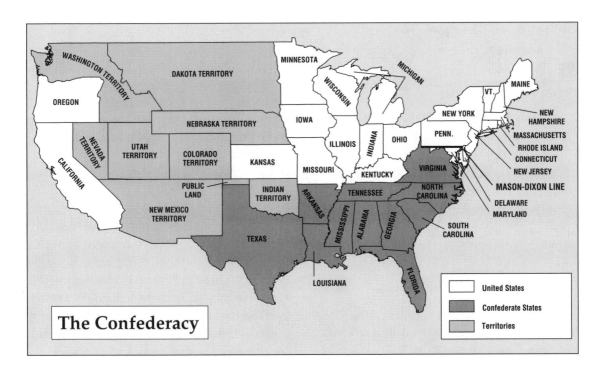

The Confederacy

	United States
	Confederate States
	Territories

HABEAS CORPUS

A writ of habeas corpus *is an order by a judge to have a prisoner brought to court to determine the legality of the imprisonment.*

Abraham Lincoln was the only U.S. president ever to suspend the writ of habeas corpus, *even temporarily. These controversial actions have led some to call him a dictator, and historians still debate whether his actions were justified. In* The Fate of Liberty: Abraham Lincoln and Civil Liberties, *Mark E. Neely Jr. gives a brief history:*

Habeas corpus had been important to the founders of the country and owned a hallowed place in American law and myth long before there was an active antislavery movement. It was a part of the American birthright. Historian Milton Cantor points out that though it was not regarded as a natural right, the writ of *habeas corpus* was the only common-law process mentioned in the United States Constitution, surely an index of its importance in the eyes of the country's founders. The delegates to the constitutional convention at first voted unanimously that "the privilege of the writ of Habeas Corpus shall not be suspended." Later, Gouverneur Morris introduced a qualifying clause adapted from the Massachusetts constitution: "unless in cases of rebellion or invasion the public safety may require it." In qualified form, then, the provision passed by a vote of seven states to three and became part of Article I, Section 9.

largely because the war itself was unprecedented, unparalleled in American history. Moreover, the executive gained power because only executive action was possible between the fall of Fort Sumter and 4 July.[45]

ADDITIONAL EMERGENCY MEASURES

In essence, Lincoln reasoned that as chief executive, he had the duty to manage as he saw fit, with little help or interference from the other branches of the government. And to fulfill this constitutional obligation as commander in chief, particularly under emergency conditions, Lincoln believed he could utilize (some would say usurp) powers that usually resided in the legislative branch. Without prior approval from Congress, he proclaimed a blockade, extended the period for voluntary enlistment to three years, increased the size of the army and navy, and entrusted public funds to private persons for the purchase of arms and supplies.

To garner congressional approval for these unprecedented actions, Lincoln sent an explanation to the special session of Congress he had earlier summoned for July 4. This justification, included in his message to Congress on that symbolic day, was also intended for the American people:

President Lincoln, as head of the executive branch of government, also utilized powers normally accorded by the Constitution to Congress. Considering his actions to be emergency measures, he then expected Congress to ratify them later.

These measures, whether strictly legal or not, were ventured upon, under what appeared to be a popular demand, and a public necessity; trusting, then, as now, that Congress would readily ratify them. It is believed that nothing has been done beyond the constitutional competency of Congress.[46]

In *The Presidency of Abraham Lincoln*, Paludan offered this analysis:

It was, as Herman Belz notes, "a new and remarkable doctrine" that the president could use powers that the Constitution gave to Congress and then expect congressmen to *later* ratify executive action.[47]

REASONS FOR THE SUSPENSION OF CIVIL LIBERTIES

Most of Lincoln's "extraconstitutional" emergency measures were approved by Congress retroactively, but he had no policy on civil liberties. Whenever there was an emergency or threatening situation, Lincoln would respond with a new proclamation suspending the writ of *habeas corpus* in that locality, until by September 1862 the entire nation had lost that civil liberty. Tens of thousands of civilians were arrested and put in military prisons in the North, if only for brief periods. Generally speaking, citizens were deprived of their civil liberties for reasons of national security, despite claims by Lincoln's opponents that the president was attempting to manipulate political events. Most of the first detainees were spies, smugglers, blockade runners, carriers of contraband, and foreign nationals. A few were political prisoners. The purpose of the first suspension of the writ of *habeas corpus* was clearly to keep the route to the capital open for military reinforcements. It was not political, and the use of the suspension never became primarily political. The Democratic Party maintained Lincoln's policies were aimed specifically at them because they were political opponents, but the evidence does not support this claim. Lincoln did, however, put thousands of civilians under military arrest throughout the war to prevent secession when it seemed imminent and thus to preserve the Union.

6 Commander in Chief

Because of the emergency situation, Lincoln's role as commander in chief was his most demanding and absorbing. Because he had little military experience and had never studied the principles and tactics of warfare, he was once again obliged to educate himself and learn by doing.

BATTLE OF BULL RUN

With the ninety-day term of Lincoln's original call for militia soon to expire and Union pressure for an offensive building, the president knew he had to engage the Confederate forces before the end of the summer of 1861. Inexperienced and optimistic, Lincoln believed one victory would end the war. In July, he ordered an advance against the Confederate army near Manassas, Virginia, only twenty-five miles from Washington, D.C. When Lincoln ordered that advance on the Rebels, he expected an easy victory. But Union troops, under General Irvin McDowell, delayed a week after authorization to move. This gave the Confederacy time to send more troops, and the ill-prepared Union troops were forced to re-treat, suffering a disastrous defeat: 460 Union soldiers were dead and more than 2,000 wounded and missing. This engagement became known as the first battle of Bull Run. A year later, the Confederates would gain another victory on the same battlefield.

The Union would surely have won if McDowell had attacked before the arrival of the unanticipated Confederate reinforcements. But Lincoln, as commander in chief, assumed the blame. Assessing the situation, he then appointed General George B. McClellan to take charge of the Union forces around the capital (later named the Army of the Potomac) and to train the more than one hundred thousand untrained volunteers he would command by November.

LINCOLN AND McCLELLAN

The appointment of McClellan to head the Army of the Potomac was the beginning of a rocky relationship that worsened as the war dragged on. The general and the president were opposites in nearly every respect: appearance, demeanor,

General George McClellan's appointment by Lincoln to head the Army of the Potomac was disastrous. The general refused to take his troops into battle.

tion. He frequently visited McClellan's headquarters to read dispatches, discuss campaigns, and make strategic suggestions, but McClellan refused to advance, asserting the troops were not ready, convinced he knew better than the commander in chief.

THE WEIGHT OF THE WAR

Lincoln's frustration continued to grow and, having borrowed and hastily read books on military tactics from the Library of Congress, he felt he must step in. On January 27, 1862, he published the "President's General War Order No. 1," which ordered all the U.S. land and naval forces to advance on or before February 22, former President George Washington's birthday. In effect he was warning them that they must act. Four days later he issued another order directing the Army of the Potomac to advance and seize Manassas on or before February 22. His plan, as he explained it, was to "threaten all their positions at the same time with superior force, and if they weakened one to strengthen another, seize and hold that one."[49] Lincoln's plan revealed his inexperience; it ignored crucial intelligence-related considerations such as readiness of the troops, weather, roads, communications, and the tenacity of the Confederate army.

The overwhelming responsibility was beginning to weigh on Lincoln. It was his war, and he was in charge of it. But it was not going the way he wanted it to. Lincoln was distressed by the deaths and maiming, the agonized families, on both sides,

upbringing, education, character, ideology—and McClellan was convinced that he was Lincoln's superior in every regard. McClellan, age thirty-five, a staunch Democrat and a skilled engineer who had graduated second in his class from the U.S. Military Academy at West Point, did not respect Lincoln, referring to him as a "gorilla" and a "well-meaning baboon."[48] Excellent at preparing troops, McClellan was popular and revered by the men, but by January 1862 he still had not taken the troops into battle. The North badly needed a victory and Lincoln wanted acby the toll it was taking on his beloved country. It was taking its toll on his private life, too. He had little time or energy to comfort and support his wife as she struggled to raise their young children. She turned to shopping and refurbishing the White House as an escape and a diversion, running up exorbitant bills, further worrying the president.

PERSONAL ANGUISH

To add to his burden, eleven-year-old Willie died in February after a short bout with typhoid fever, devastating both parents and dealing Mary a blow from which she would never recover. She could not bring herself to attend her son's funeral or ever again enter his room. She was essentially bedridden for three months. Lincoln was suffering, too. When he had looked at Willie's face after he died, he could barely speak, "It is hard, hard to have him die. . . . Willie was too good for this earth . . . but then we loved him so."[50] Upon seeing Lincoln, a friend said, "I never saw a man so bowed down with grief,"[51] and he could often be heard weeping alone in one of the empty rooms.

The death of the family's youngest son Willie (second from left) from typhoid fever devastated Lincoln and left Mary forever grief stricken.

But Lincoln dealt with his anguish in other ways. He found some comfort in caring for Tad, who was recovering from the same illness, which the children had caught as a result of pollution in the White House water system. And he found consolation in spirituality. Although he did not belong to any church or adhere to any particular doctrine, after he became president, he increasingly turned to God to ask for assistance and mentioned the Creator in speeches. And now, rather than abstract invocations of the Almighty or pleas to the Divine Being to save the Union, he needed explicit help to get him through this personal tragedy. Lincoln talked with Reverend Phineas D. Gurley, pastor of the New York Avenue Presbyterian Church in Washington, D.C., who assured him Willie was not dead, but alive in heaven.

Later, Lincoln would say that at this time in his life he underwent "a process of crystallization"[52] in his religious beliefs. It is not clear exactly what he meant by that statement, since even then he did not join any Christian denomination nor reject his fatalism. But he was able to see and feel beyond his own pain and realize that a large part of the country was also in mourning. So many families had also lost sons, and he was grieving with them, too. In addition to personal tragedies, the president became locked in combat with one of his own generals.

McClellan's Plan

Because of his arrogance and mistrust, McClellan had kept his overall strategy from his subordinates, from Congress, and even from the president. Finally, the President's General War Order No. 1 forced McClellan to reveal his plan to Lincoln. He believed advancing on Manassas, as Lincoln had ordered, would be a disaster and that the Union army's goal should be to capture Richmond, the Confederate capital. His plan was to attack Richmond from the east, where the navy could protect his line of supplies, fight, forcing a surrender and ending the war. Lincoln was opposed to the plan from the beginning, and that would be a major source of friction between them, particularly given McClellan's vanity and haughtiness, which often bordered on insubordination.

Having become increasingly more interested and active in military affairs as time passed and the war effort faltered, Lincoln made frequent late-night visits to McClellan's house to discuss strategy. On one occasion, McClellan decided to put a stop to these visits and to what he considered meddling by an inferior. Presidential Secretary John Hay wrote this account of the encounter:

> I wish here to record what I consider a portent of evil to come. The president, [Secretary of State William H.] Seward, and I went over to McClellan's house. After we had waited an hour, McClellan came in and went upstairs, passing the room where the president and secretary of state were seated. They waited about half an hour and sent once more a servant to tell the general they were

"The President Is an Idiot"

George B. McClellan, appointed commander in chief of the Army of the Potomac at thirty-five, was a graduate of West Point, bright, gallant, a brilliant organizer and trainer who inspired his troops. He was also self-absorbed, stubborn, arrogant, and disrespectful. Lincoln had trouble with him from the beginning. The general did not conceal his contempt for his commander in chief, as can be seen in excerpts from letters written to his wife from the field found in Lincoln: As I Knew Him.

August 16, 1861: The president is an idiot. . . .

October 11, 1861: The president is nothing more than a well meaning baboon.

November 17, 1861: I went to the White House shortly after tea where I found *"the original gorilla,"* about as intelligent as ever. What a specimen to be at the head of our affairs now!

April 8, 1862: The President very coolly telegraphed me yesterday that he thought I had better break the enemy's lines at once! I was much tempted to reply that he had better come and do it himself.

October 29, 1862: If you could know the mean and dirty character of the dispatches [from Lincoln] I receive you would boil over with anger. . . . But the good of the country requires me to submit to all this from men whom I know to be greatly my inferiors socially, intellectually and morally! There never was a truer epithet applied to a certain individual than that of the "Gorilla."

Lincoln visits General McClellan and his staff. The general's poor military judgment, arrogance, and blatant contempt for the president finally led to his dismissal from the army.

"I Recognized His Great Ability"

Ulysses S. Grant did not meet Lincoln until March 1864, when he was called to the capital to receive his commission as lieutenant general. By that time, Grant was already a Union war hero. Lincoln was grateful and relieved, after having suffered a series of poor leaders. There was a great deal of mutual respect, admiration, and appreciation.

This excerpt is from Grant's autobiography. He wrote it while suffering from cancer to provide for his family, because his finances were in ruin. He completed it just before he died and did not see it become a tremendous bestseller.

I had also read the remarkable series of debates between Lincoln and Douglas a few years before, when they were rival candidates for the United States Senate. I was then a resident of Missouri, and by no means a "Lincoln man" in that contest, but I recognized then his great ability.

In my first interview with Mr. Lincoln alone he stated to me that he had never professed to be a military man or to know how campaigns should be conducted, and never wanted to interfere in them; but that procrastination on the part of commanders, and the pressure from the people at the North and from Congress, which was always with him, forced him into issuing his series of "Military Orders"—No. 1, No. 2, No. 3, etc. [He did not know that they were not all wrong, and did know that some of them were.] All he wanted, or had ever wanted, was some one who would take the responsibility and act and call on him for all the assistance needed; he would pledge himself to use all the power of the Government in rendering such assistance. Assuring him that I would do the best I could with the means at hand, and avoid as far as possible annoying him or the War Department, our first interview ended.

---

there. And the answer came back that the general had gone to bed. I merely record this unparalleled insolence without comment.[53]

Lincoln brushed off the incident, convinced it was not the time to focus on etiquette, but he was losing confidence in McClellan. And he made no more visits to his house.

Lincoln's Grasp of Military Matters Grows

Lincoln was now very involved with military developments and out of necessity was gaining a grasp of war, that is, a comprehension of military theory and command structure. In *Recollections of the Civil War with the Leaders at Washington and in the Field in the Sixties*, Charles A. Dana, a newspaper editor and publisher who had been an assistant secretary in the War Department, described how adept Lincoln became:

> Another interesting fact about Abraham Lincoln is that he developed into a great military man; that is to say, a man of supreme military judgment. I do not risk anything in saying that if one will study the records of the war and study the writings relating to it, he will agree with me that the greatest general we had, greater than [Ulysses S.] Grant [ultimately general in chief of the Union armies] or [George H.] Thomas [victor, late in the war, in major engagements in Tennessee], was Abraham Lincoln. It was not so at the beginning; but after three or four years of constant practice in the science and art of war, he arrived at this extraordinary knowledge of it. . . . To sum it up, he was a born leader of men. He knew human nature; he knew what chord to strike, and was never afraid to strike it when he believed the time had arrived.[54]

Lincoln's increased knowledge and skill fueled his frustration with what he saw as procrastination on the part of commanders, particularly McClellan. At one point, in early 1862, Lincoln even thought of leading one of the armies into battle himself as commander in chief, but he knew he was no military man and that was merely his frustration—and a fantasy. "All he wanted or had ever wanted," General Grant once recalled, "was some-

one who would take responsibility and act, and call on him for all the assistance needed, he would pledge himself to use all the power of government in rendering such assistance."[55]

NORTH AND SOUTH: STRENGTHS AND WEAKNESSES

The war raged on, but it was not going well for Lincoln. Despite what appeared to be the Union's overwhelming advantages, the Confederacy was often able to counteract them. The North's population

The great general Ulysses S. Grant. Lincoln's leadership prowess and his superb military judgment may have surpassed even Grant's abilities.

FATHER ABRAHAM

Noah Brooks, the Washington correspondent for the Sacramento Daily Union, *was one of Lincoln's favorite journalists and probably would have been named to replace outgoing White House private secretary John Nicolay if Lincoln had not been assassinated. He had broad access to the White House, and as quoted in* Lincoln As I Knew Him, *offers a close-up view of the president at work:*

When the president lives in town he commences his day's work long before the city is astir, and before breakfast he consumes two hours or more in writing, reading, or studying some of the host of subjects which he has on hand. . . . Breakfast over, by nine o'clock he has directed that the gate which lets in the people shall be opened upon him, and then the multitude of cards, notes, and messages which are in the hands of his usher come upon him. . . . The President sits at his table and kindly greets whoever comes. . . . In his anxiety to do equal and exact justice to all, he excludes or delays those who might see him sooner if he did not try to do so much. No man has a kinder heart than Abraham Lincoln, and all who meet him go away thoroughly impressed with the preponderance of those two lovable and noble traits of his character.

was about two and a half times that of the South: 22 million in the twenty-three Union states to 9 million (more than 3 million slaves) in the eleven Confederate states, and it had about four times as many men available to fight. The North had more money, more industry, more railroads, a superior navy, and a superior agricultural system.

The South, however, stood its ground with the defensive advantage of fighting on its own soil, a loyal and committed populace fiercely fighting for its homeland and way of life, and better generals. Poor military leadership was a problem for the North from the beginning. But as Lincoln gained knowledge and experi-

ence as commander in chief, he became more skilled at selecting his commanders and in drawing out the best performances they were able to give.

The Confederacy also had an advantage in the physical layout of the combat arena. In what is known as the concept of interior and exterior lines, the imaginary line dividing the Confederacy and the Union was seen as a big circular arc, a half-circle with its rounded edge lying to the north. To attack the South, Union forces theoretically had to travel to points on the semicircle, and Confederate forces, needing to send reinforcements or protect a given area, could move along the shorter paths inside the arc.

THE WAR DRAGS ON

Contrary to the early expectations of most Northerners, the war was anything but short and easy. Ulysses S. Grant, also a West Point graduate, provided a glimmer of hope when he captured Fort Henry and Fort Donelson in February 1862, opening vital arteries into the South and delivering the first major Union victory. When the Confederate commander had asked for terms, Grant responded, "No terms except an unconditional and immediate surrender can be accepted."[56] Brigadier general of volunteers at the time, Grant was immediately promoted to major general and now ranked second in the West. The administration was once again op-

timistic and believed the Confederacy could be defeated with one big push from the Army of the Potomac.

The optimism was short-lived, however, because after that initial victory, the armies in the Mississippi Valley seemed stuck, unable to advance. And the Army of the Potomac could not provide that one big push. It became apparent that defeating the Confederacy would not be a simple task. Like many coming to that realization, Grant's thinking changed when he was finally victorious after a surprise Confederate attack at Shiloh, Tennessee, in April. After a two-day battle that he almost lost—and thirteen thousand Union and eleven thousand Confederate casualties—he realized

General Grant (left center) at the Battle of Shiloh. The confrontation was one of the war's bloodiest, resulting in over ten thousand casualties each for the Union and Confederate armies.

that a limited war was impossible, and the only way he would be able to save the Union was by complete conquest. That was a costly lesson. Shiloh was the bloodiest battle to that time: More Americans died there than in the Revolutionary War, the War of 1812, and the Mexican War combined. Because of his unpreparedness, many blamed Grant for the losses and wanted him removed. But Lincoln was steadfast, "I can't spare this man; he fights."[57]

INCREASED FRUSTRATION WITH McCLELLAN

General McClellan remained a source of frustration to the president. The haughty West Pointer continually made excuses for not advancing and complained constantly. Repeatedly he claimed that his troops were not ready, that he was overpowered by superior numbers, and that he needed reinforcements. Lincoln, who ultimately doubted that McClellan would ever fight a significant battle to take Richmond, offered this balanced but damning characterization of his general: He "had the capacity to make arrangements properly for a great conflict, but as the hour for action approached he became nervous and oppressed with the responsibility and hesitated to meet the crisis."[58]

In May 1862 McClellan was approaching Richmond, and it looked like victory was finally within reach. But he stopped six miles away, again demanding reinforcements. Historian James MacPherson explained McClellan's inability to move

General Robert E. Lee is pictured at his home shortly after the Civil War ended. Lincoln had hoped the brilliant general would lead the Union army, but Lee chose to join the Confederacy.

his troops in *Abraham and Mary Lincoln: A House Divided* (PBS):

> The trouble with McClellan was that he was psychologically unable to commit this mechanism [the Army of the Potomac], that he had created, to battle. He was afraid that having created this wonderful machine, if he started it up, that he might destroy it.[59]

Finally, in June, after receiving additional troops, McClellan was preparing to advance on Richmond when a new Confederate commander, Robert E. Lee, attacked the Army of the Potomac first. In 1861 Lee, a brilliant general, had declined an offer made on Lincoln's behalf to command the Union Army. Indeed, he had resigned from the U.S. Army when Virginia, his home state, seceded. McClellan, who had continually overestimated the number and strength of Confederate troops, underestimated Lee. In a series of battles from June 26 to July 1, Lee forced McClellan to retreat. It had been almost four months, and McClellan had gained nothing. He refused to admit defeat, saying he just had failed to win, blaming "superior numbers."[60] McClellan did not threaten Richmond again.

COMMANDER IN CHIEF

During this time, Lincoln was extremely distraught and had great difficulty eating and sleeping. He lost weight and looked worried and weary. The certainty of a long war was taking its toll.

Although Lincoln was initially inexperienced and insecure about military matters, he never went to his cabinet or other politicians for advice. He believed the commander in chief was the one—the only one—in control, and as the president, that was his duty. He also chose the highest-ranking generals without advice or assistance, and he developed considerable insight and skill in knowing how to best approach individual commanders and specific situations. In *The Last Best Hope of Earth*, Mark E. Neely Jr. wrote that Lincoln might not have been a military genius, "But as commander in chief, who must combine military perception with political vision and the skillful handling of personalities, Lincoln had no superior in American history."[61]

7 The Great Emancipator

Lincoln expanded the powers of the commander in chief to manage a war that threatened the Union. Those powers also helped to solve the problem that caused the rebellion, secession, and Civil War: slavery. The Emancipation Proclamation was the first step in abolishing that institution by freeing the slaves in the rebelling states. Because he authored and enacted it, Abraham Lincoln is known as the Great Emancipator. But before he was able to decide that he had constitutional authority to free the slaves, his views had to evolve.

INCREASING PRESSURE FOR EMANCIPATION

Early in his presidency, Lincoln had upheld his campaign promise not to interfere with the institution of slavery where it already existed. In 1861, he thought that because slaves were considered to be the property of their owners, any presidential proclamation abolishing slavery would be unconstitutional, an act of dictatorship.

Yet Lincoln had always been opposed to slavery on moral and philosophical grounds. As a legislator, he had condemned it publicly as "founded on both injustice and bad policy"[62] as early as 1837. But with emancipation seemingly ruled out, his problem was how to eliminate the institution of slavery itself. And there were increasing external pressures that were nudging him. Religious groups were calling for an end to what many saw as the "venom of slavery." Abolitionists such as Henry Ward Beecher, Horace Greeley, Susan B. Anthony, and Angelina Grimke Weld were becoming increasingly vocal in their demands for emancipation. The drumbeat for some form of military service for blacks was intensifying in the North, especially among abolitionists. Frederick Douglass, a former slave and one of the most influential and eloquent abolitionists, appealed for the use of black soldiers, asserting that the "Union cause would never prosper till the war assumed an Anti-Slavery attitude, and the Negro was enlisted on the loyal side."[63] And in the South, though slaves were not in the military, they were being used against the Union by taking over some of their owners' civilian responsibilities, which freed the white Southerners to join the uniformed Confederate forces.

PRESSURE FROM THE MILITARY

There was pressure from the ranks of the Union army as well. In December 1861 Simon Cameron, Lincoln's first secretary of war, sent a report to Lincoln recommending that Southern slaves who had escaped to the Union lines should be emancipated and armed to be used against the rebels. But that was not all: He

Former slave Frederick Douglass was an important and deeply committed abolitionist.

sent the report to the postmasters and newspapers of the larger cities, infuriating the president. After Lincoln demanded that the report be recalled and Cameron's remarks about the slaves removed, he sent a letter to Cameron informing him that he was being nominated for the post of the U.S. minister to Russia. Cameron was so insulted by the letter that Lincoln withdrew it and allowed Cameron to resign, replacing him with Edwin Stanton as secretary of war.

In late August 1861, Major General John C. Frémont declared martial law in Missouri. Under martial law, all civilians bearing arms would be tried by court martial, and shot if convicted. In addition, all the slaves taken from those resisting the authority of the United States would be emancipated. This action not only violated the provisions of the First Confiscation Act (August 6, 1861), which had established official procedures for seizing slaves who helped the rebel army, but was in opposition to Lincoln's policy of dealing cautiously with border slave states. It did not sit well with Lincoln and with many others. Volunteers on several fronts refused to fight if Frémont's order was in effect, so Lincoln ordered Frémont to conform to the provisions of the Confiscation Act concerning slavery and emancipation and to refrain from implementing the extreme measures he had announced.

Then in May 1862 Major General David Hunter, another Union officer and commander of the Department of the South (composed of Georgia, Florida, and South Carolina), proclaimed that "slavery and martial law in a free country are altogether incompatible."[64] He then decreed slaves free throughout the Department of the South. Lincoln declared Hunter's proclamation "altogether void" and made certain everyone understood that only the president could determine whether or not slaves would be set free. This represented a significant change in Lincoln's thinking: He now was convinced that the president, as commander in chief, could issue an emancipation proclamation as a military necessity and that the Constitution would allow abolition to save the Union from destruction in war.

PRESSURE FROM CONGRESS

In an attempt to demonstrate its authority, Congress had enacted legislation that moved steadily closer to emancipation. The First Confiscation Act provided that when slave owners used their slaves to directly assist them with the rebellion, their claim to the labor of those slaves was forfeited. This act was a step toward emancipation under specific circumstances. This measure, passed in August 1861, would affect only slaves used by the South for solely military purposes.

In 1862 the pace quickened. In April Congress passed a law abolishing slavery in the District of Columbia. Lincoln insisted on adding compensation to masters and providing for the resettlement of the freedmen. (He believed that gradual emancipation was better for everyone and that voluntary emancipation by owners would be more enduring than forced freedom.) In June, Congress passed a bill abolishing slavery in the territories. Then in July, it passed the Second Confiscation Act, which provided that the slaves of anyone convicted of treason would be free and that the slaves of all persons supporting rebellion, once they came under control of the army, would be "forever free of their servitude, and not again held as slaves." The act also authorized the president to employ as many blacks as necessary for the suppression of the rebellion. The president opposed the act, remarking to an Illinois Senator, "It is startling to say that congress can free a slave within a state. Congress has no power over slavery in the states."[65] He was persuaded to sign it, but he intended to act first with his own plan for emancipation. On the same day he also signed the Militia Act, which let blacks fill state militia quotas and provided that any enemy-owned slave who performed military service would be free, as would his wife, children, and mother.

THE ROOT OF LINCOLN'S RESISTANCE

Lincoln's initial resistance to emancipation had stemmed from two things he held dear: the Constitution and the Union. He had believed that although individuals could and should free their own slaves, there was no constitutional support for unilateral emancipation, particularly without compensation to the owners. And as much as he abhorred and wanted to eliminate slavery, preserving the Union was his major goal. If he could not do that and win the war, he would not be able to abolish slavery or accomplish any of his other goals.

WORKING TOWARD EMANCIPATION

As early as November 1861, Lincoln had started working on a bill for compensated emancipation. In March 1862, after working for three months by himself, he made what amounted to his first formal proposal concerning the abolishment of slavery when he sent to Congress a special message on gradual, compensated emancipation. He also believed that the Southern states would realize the futility of continuing to fight when the program to free slaves by purchase began. It would be a first step against slavery that would destroy hope in the Confederacy and thus substantially end the rebellion. And on a purely practical level, paying to free the slaves would cost much less than fighting a war. Lincoln, for the first time, linked emancipation with the war effort.

Pressure from Congress, military officers, abolitionists, religious groups, and increasingly pro-emancipation public

An illustration depicts President Lincoln working on the controversial Emancipation Proclamation.

opinion in the North, forced Lincoln to scrutinize his position and take further action. Meanwhile, thousands of slaves were unwilling to wait for emancipation and in increasing numbers crossed Confederate lines into Union territory, hiding in Union army camps or living in crowded refugee camps.

And pressure was mounting from the battlefield. For the Union, the war was worsening. They had not brought the Confederacy to its knees because they had not dealt a blow to its heart. By spring of 1862, it was clear that because the issue of slavery was at the heart of the rebellion and the practice of slavery sustained the Confederacy, freeing the slaves and ending slavery was necessary to win the war and to save the Union. Now Lincoln had a military reason to free the slaves—one he thought the North would accept. Moreover, he was convinced that the Constitution allowed the president, as commander in chief, to free the slaves as a military necessity to save the Union from destruction in war. So now his two problems of military victory and slavery were intertwined under his powers as commander in chief. He decided to issue an Emancipation Proclamation.

MOVES TOWARD EMANCIPATION

Without anyone's help or knowledge, Abraham Lincoln set in motion what would become one of the most important, revered, and controversial acts in history and one of his greatest accomplishments and contributions.

But, as was often the case, Lincoln did not give any indication that a decision had been made or that there had been a shift in his thinking. In fact, he continued to publicly work for gradual compensated emancipation while he was privately working on the proclamation. He even had some fun with it, according to David Herbert Donald, in his book *Lincoln*:

> During June and July when Lincoln was drafting an emancipation order, he often played a kind of game with the numerous visitors who descended on him to urge him to free the slaves. The measures they advocated were precisely those that he was attempting to formulate in his document at the War Department. If he challenged their arguments, he was, in effect, testing his own.[66]

In July, after once again appealing for compensated emancipation, Lincoln revealed his plan to two surprised cabinet secretaries. Then on July 22, he called a meeting of the full cabinet to tell his advisors of his decision to issue an emancipation proclamation. The preliminary proclamation said that the war would continue for the Union, that efforts would continue to buy, set free, and colonize slaves in the border states and that on January 1, 1863, all slaves in states or parts of states in rebellion against the United States "shall be then, thenceforward, and forever free" and the federal government would "recognize the freedom of such persons."[67] Lincoln was persuaded, however, not to issue a proclamation immediately. Secretary of State Seward argued

RESPONSE TO HORACE GREELEY

Lincoln felt it necessary to keep his decision to issue an Emancipation Proclamation secret. In a public response to an editorial, "The Prayer of Twenty Millions," by New York Tribune *editor Horace Greeley, Lincoln continued to give the impression—long after he had made the decision and just a month before he issued the proclamation— that he didn't intend to free the slaves. His response is reprinted in* Abraham Lincoln: His Speeches and Writings:

I would save the Union. . . . If there be those who would not save the Union, unless they could at the same time *save* slavery, I do not agree with them. If there be those who would not save the Union unless they could at the same time *destroy* slavery, I do not agree with them. My paramount object in this struggle *is* to save the Union, and is *not* either to save or to destroy slavery. If I could save the Union without freeing *any* slave I would do it, and if I could save it by freeing *all* the slaves I would do it; and if I could save it by freeing some and leaving others alone I would also do that. What I do about slavery, and the colored race, I do because I believe it helps to save the Union; and what I forbear, I forbear because I do *not* believe it would help to save the Union. . . . I have here stated my purpose according to my view of *official* duty; and I intend no modification of my oft-expressed *personal* wish that all men every where could be free.

adamantly that it was essential to wait until after a military success, for otherwise, with the Union having suffered so many military defeats, the freeing of Southern slaves would look like a "last measure of an exhausted government, a cry for help."[68]

PLANS FOR THE AFTERMATH OF EMANCIPATION

There was much planning to be done before emancipation could be proclaimed.

Lincoln was concerned about what would happen to the slaves when they were free. Believing whites and blacks could not live together, he was in favor of sending former slaves to Africa, as well as to the Caribbean and Central America.

He called a delegation of black leaders—the first ever—to the White House to present his plan of deportation and colonization. Frederick Douglass was outraged by the plan and critical of Lincoln for supporting it. "The genuine spark of humanity is missing in it," he asserted. "No sincere wish to improve the condition of the oppressed has dictated it. It expresses merely the desire to get rid of them."[69] Douglass, whom Lincoln considered "one of the most meritorious men in America,"[70] would later reflect on Lincoln's attitude toward blacks and put his struggle with emancipation in context in the 1888 *Reminiscences of Abraham Lincoln by Distinguished Men of His Time:*

> In all my interviews with Mr. Lincoln I was impressed with his entire freedom from popular prejudice against the colored race. He was the first great man that I talked with in the United States freely, who in no single instance reminded me of the difference between himself and myself, of the difference of color, and I thought that all the more remarkable because he came from a State where there were black laws. I account partially for his kindness to me because of the similarity with which I had fought my way up, we both starting at the lowest round of the ladder. . . .
>
> Viewed from the genuine abolition ground, Mr. Lincoln seemed tardy, cold, dull, and indifferent; but measuring him by the sentiment of his country, a sentiment he was bound as a statesman to consult, he was swift, zealous, radical, and determined.[71]

THE EXCRUCIATING WAIT

The next two months were difficult for Lincoln. The preliminary proclamation was written, but he was waiting for a victory to issue it. By late August, he thought the time had come. Union troops were advancing toward Manassas and Lincoln was confident they would defeat Lee's men at the second battle of Bull Run. But he was wrong, the Confederate troops were victorious. And once again, they threatened Washington. Lincoln's intent to fight an offensive war had been thwarted, and the Union was back on the defensive.

Lincoln was depressed, demoralized, and once again fatalistic. Victory, emancipation, the Union—everything seemed out of his grasp. He wrote in a memorandum to himself, "I am almost ready to say that God wills this contest, and wills that it shall not end yet."[72] It seemed to him that God had a purpose, different from his or Lee's, and he did not know what it was.

But the president understood that his troops were demoralized, too. He knew that to restore morale and reorganize the Army of the Potomac, he needed to reinstate McClellan, despite the known weaknesses of the arrogant general, who was despised by most of Lincoln's advisors.

Under increasing pressure from some partisan supporters to revert to his original policy of noninterference with slavery where it existed, because they feared losing the upcoming elections, and from the public for an emancipation order, Lincoln said, "It is my earnest desire to know the will of Providence [God] in this matter. *And if I can learn what it is I will do it!*" He wanted a sign, and he later told the cabinet that he had "made a vow, a covenant,

MEDITATION ON THE DIVINE WILL

John Hay, Lincoln's presidential secretary, found and made a copy of the following meditation, which was not intended for the public eye. Always fatalistic, after Willie's death Lincoln contemplated divine will, or Providence, even more. This extract was written in 1862 after several major Union defeats and is found in Lincoln *by David Herbert Donald.*

The will of God prevails. In great contests each party claims to act in accordance with the will of God. Both *may* be, and one *must* be wrong. God can not be *for*, and *against* the same thing at the same time. In the present civil war it is quite possible that God's purpose is something different from the purpose of either party—and yet human instrumentalities, working just as they do, are of the best adaptation to effect His purpose. I am almost ready to say this is probably true—that God wills this contest, and wills that it shall not end yet. By this mere quiet power, on the minds of the now contestants, He could have either saved or *destroyed* the Union without a human contest. Yet the contest began. And having begun He could give the final victory to either side any day. Yet the contest proceeds.

that if God gave us the victory in the approaching battle, he would consider it an indication of Divine will, and that it was his duty to move forward in the cause of emancipation."[73]

On September 17, 1862, the military victory—and the omen—Lincoln desperately needed was finally realized. At Antietam Creek in Maryland, McClellan's Army of the Potomac defeated the Confederates in an exceptionally bloody battle. On both sides, almost six thousand were killed and seventeen thousand wounded with thousands missing in what remains the largest number of American casualties in a single day in U.S. history. It was a terrible victory.

THE PRELIMINARY EMANCIPATION PROCLAMATION

When Lincoln received news of the victory, he was determined to wait no longer. He was staying in the presidential cottage at the Soldiers' Home (a veterans' retirement home, situated about three miles from the capital, which served as the summer White House, away from the heat), and there he finished writing the second draft of the preliminary proclamation. Three days later, on Saturday, he went to Washington and called the cabinet together to read it. On Monday, September 22, the Preliminary Emancipation Proclamation was issued, and the text was

The Army of the Potomac, under the command of General George McClellan, engages Confederate soldiers at the bloody Battle of Antietam in September 1862.

printed in newspapers across the country. It read:

> That on the first day of January in the year of our Lord, one thousand eight hundred and sixty-three, all persons held as slaves within any state, or designated part of a state, the people whereof shall be in rebellion against the United States shall be then, thenceforward, and forever free. . . .[74]

Almost 3 million slaves—all those living where citizens rebelled—would be "forever free." That was more than 82 percent of the slaves in the Confederacy and 74 percent in the United States.

REACTION TO THE PROCLAMATION

Initial public reaction to the proclamation was favorable. The influential *New York Tribune* editor Horace Greeley, long an outspoken abolitionist, wrote in his newspaper that "in all ages there has been no act of one man and of one people so sublime as this emancipation of a race—no act so fraught with good for the sons of men in all time to come."[75] Most contemporary liberals praised the proclamation, as did most blacks. Frederick Douglass said, "We shout for joy that we live to record this righteous decree."[76] Most abolitionists were jubilant. Respected literary figures such as poet Walt Whitman and essayist Ralph Waldo Emerson believed it was a new birth of freedom, a path to union, hope, and achieving ideals.

However, opposition in the South was vehement. The front-page article in the Richmond *Examiner* stated:

> It will have no effect on the South; its only serious importance is its indication that the North will stop at nothing in prosecuting the War . . . a call for the insurrection of four million slaves [the approximate number of slaves in the United States], and the inauguration of a reign of hell upon earth.[77]

And some newspapers, such as the Richmond *Enquirer*, rather than attacking the proclamation, attacked Lincoln "as black of soul as the vilest of the train [of abolitionists] whose behests he is obeying. So far as he can do so, he has devoted the Southern Confederacy to the Direst destruction that can befall a people."[78] Opposition, as expected, was widespread, and the Democrats overwhelmingly won the midterm elections of 1862.

BENDING UNDER THE WEIGHT

A midterm political loss was the least of Lincoln's many worries. It appeared that he, as one observer noted, was "literally bending under the weight of his

ANNUAL MESSAGE TO CONGRESS DECEMBER 1, 1862

One month before the Emancipation Proclamation would take effect, in his second annual message, Lincoln dealt mainly with slavery in loyal states—a plan for compensated, gradual emancipation and colonization of freedmen. The closing paragraph, reprinted from Abraham Lincoln: His Speeches and Writings, *is one of Lincoln's most eloquent.*

Fellow citizens, *we* cannot escape history. We of this Congress and this administration will be remembered in spite of ourselves. No personal significance, or insignificance, can spare one or another of us. The fiery trial through which we pass, will light us down, in honor or dishonor, to the latest generation. We *say* we are for the Union. The world will not forget that we say this. We know how to save the Union. The world knows we do know how to save it. We—even *we here*—hold the power, and bear the responsibility. In *giving* freedom to the *slave* we *assure* freedom to the *free*—honorable alike in what we give, and what we preserve. We shall nobly save, or meanly lose, the last best hope of earth. Other means may succceed; this could not fail. The way is plain, peaceful, generous, just—a way, which, if followed, the world will forever applaud, and God must forever bless.

Final Emancipation Proclamation January 1, 1863

The final proclamation, reprinted in The Emancipation Proclamation *by John Hope Franklin, is written in legalistic prose, rather than in Lincoln's typical elegant, eloquent style. Lincoln wanted to make certain it was legally sound so that blacks could rely on it if their freedom was later challenged in court. It was a war measure issued by the commander in chief of the army. The next-to-last paragraph states that blacks could thereafter serve in the military.*

A Proclamation

Whereas, on the twenty-second day of September, in the year of our Lord one thousand eight hundred and sixty-two a proclamation was issued by the President of the United States, containing, among other things, the following, to wit:

That on the first day of January, in the year of our Lord one thousand eight hundred and sixty-three, all persons held as slaves within any state, or designated part of a state, the people whereof shall then be in rebellion against the United States, shall be then thenceforward and forever free; and the Executive Government of the United States, including the military and naval authority thereof, will recognize and maintain the freedom of such persons, and will do no act or acts to repress such persons, or any of them in any efforts they may make for their actual freedom.

. . .

And I hereby enjoin upon the people so declared to be free to abstain from all violence, unless in necessary self-defense; and I recommend to them that in all cases when allowed, they labor faithfully for reasonable wages.

And I further declare and make known, that such persons of suitable condition, will be received into the armed service of the United States to garrison forts, positions, stations and other places and to man vessels of all sorts in said service.

And upon this act sincerely believed to be an act of justice, warranted by the Constitution upon military necessity, I invoke the considerate judgment of mankind, and the gracious favor of Almighty God.

burden."[79] The war was going badly and Lincoln was bearing most of the blame while he continued to be thwarted by ineffectual generals. McClellan was still offering excuses and would not move. Lincoln saw Antietam as the beginning of an offensive, leading to the destruction of the Confederate army. He believed that McClellan had missed the perfect opportunity to chase down Lee and crush him. Extremely frustrated, Lincoln ran out of patience and again replaced McClellan.

But little more than a month later, McClellan's replacement, General Ambrose E. Burnside, disregarded the advice of the president and all officers in the area and commanded his troops to charge up Prospect Hill in Fredericksburg, Virginia, where the Confederates were waiting for them. Again and again—six times—he sent them up the hill. Even the Confederates were cheering their bravery until Burnside, in tears, finally ordered them to retreat. There were twelve thousand Union casualties. The Army of the Potomac was demoralized.

The North was outraged at the trouncing and the mounting casualties. They felt the Lincoln administration was incompetent and feared they were headed for disgrace and defeat. Lincoln was exhausted. When a friend from Springfield visited

Dignitaries gather around the president (seated, left center) for the signing of the Emancipation Proclamation.

that winter, she was shocked at Lincoln's appearance and commented, "His hair is grizzled, his gait more stooping, his countenance sallow and there's a sunken, deathly look about the large cavernous eyes. It's a lesson for human ambition to look upon."[80] But exhausted and besieged as Lincoln was, in just over two weeks he would start the new year with an act that lifted his spirits and forever changed the country.

SIGNING THE EMANCIPATION PROCLAMATION

Lincoln signed the final Emancipation Proclamation on January 1, 1863. There had been a public reception at the White House that morning where Lincoln shook hands for three hours before joining the cabinet to sign the proclamation. He looked up and commented, "I never, in my life, felt more certain that I was doing right, than I do in signing this paper."[81]

But he was concerned that his stiff, numb hand might make it appear that he wavered in his decision. Francis B. Carpenter, in residence at the White House in 1864 to paint *The First Reading of the Emancipation Proclamation to the Cabinet*, interviewed eyewitnesses and recorded the scene and Lincoln's remarks:

> I have been shaking hands since nine o'clock this morning, and my right arm is almost paralyzed. If my name ever goes into history it will be for this act, and my whole soul is in it. If my hand trembles when I sign the Proclamation, all who examine the document hereafter will say, "He hesitated."[82]

An eyewitness described what happened next: "He then turned to the table, took up his pen again, and slowly, firmly wrote the 'Abraham Lincoln' with which the whole world is now familiar. [Lincoln almost always signed "A. Lincoln."] He looked up, smiled, and said, 'That will do.'"[83]

Chapter

8 Countdown to Destiny

The Preliminary Emancipation Proclamation had been a warning to Southerners to end the rebellion before January—in one hundred days—or their slaves would be confiscated and deemed forever free. With the signing of the Emancipation Proclamation, one hundred days had passed and no Confederate state had given up the rebellion. There was open opposition to the war in the North, where many were unwilling to fight to free slaves, and in the Midwest, where antagonism toward the Proclamation was prevalent and many feared that it would lead to a heavy influx of freedmen. Volunteering almost stopped and more troops were needed, so Lincoln signed a conscription (draft) act on March 3.

THE DRAFT ACT

Its main purpose, rather than to actually draft soldiers, was to increase manpower by encouraging, inspiring, or enticing men to enlist and communities to recruit the much-needed soldiers. In that, it worked— about 1 million men volunteered during the time the draft law was in effect. The draft itself produced 170,000 soldiers:

50,000 of those called were actually drafted; 120,000 were substitutes. (It was allowable at that time for a draftee to pay a substitute $300 to take his place or the government a $300 commutation fee. This amount was about half what the average worker made per year and double the per capita income.)

The draft act was also supposed to suppress dissent. There it failed. When it went into effect it caused the worst rioting in the nation's history: the New York City draft riots of July 13–17, 1863. The working-class protestors, who resented being drafted to fight a war for emancipation, turned into angry mobs, looting, burning, and attacking soldiers, police officers, firefighters, and anyone associated with the draft process. Then they went after any blacks they could find, beating, burning, and lynching them. Troops from Gettysburg were called in to quell the riots, but before they arrived, more than one hundred people had been killed, many by hanging and burning.

BLACKS IN THE MILITARY

The results of the conscription act would not be seen for months after enactment,

Although well intentioned and largely successful, the draft act led to dissent and rioting, the worst the country had ever seen.

and more troops were needed immediately. Lincoln's position on blacks in the military had shifted, and he decided to allow their recruitment. Initially, he had been opposed to the idea, even after he issued the preliminary Emancipation Proclamation. Though the Second Confiscation Act had authorized blacks to serve in the suppression of the rebellion, Lincoln believed that because the proclamation was intended to make Confederates stop the rebellion or lose their slaves, allowing slaves who had escaped to join the Union army would undermine the proclamation's effect. Also, many people at the time believed that blacks would not fight,

and any weapons they were issued would be taken from them by the Confederates. Many others feared they would use the guns to revolt against their masters. But after pressure and persuasion from abolitionists, black leaders, some members of his cabinet, and Vice President Hamlin, Lincoln finally realized they were the greatest *"available* and yet *unavailed* of, force for restoring the Union."[84]

Significantly, two major changes in the final Emancipation Proclamation were the acceptance of former slaves into the military and the abandonment of plans for deportation. By spring, Lincoln was advocating a major recruitment of black troops.

And by the end of the war one hundred eighty thousand blacks, most emancipated slaves, had volunteered and fought bravely for the Union army.

Growing Opposition and Isolation

Nationwide, opposition to Lincoln was growing. Within his own party conservatives resented what they considered to be his transforming a war for the Union into a campaign against slavery. They also criticized executive actions such as the suspension of the writ of *habeas corpus* as unconstitutional. Radicals thought he was weak, fearful, and ignorant, and moving too slowly against slavery. Nearly everyone thought Lincoln was incompetent. Both factions of the Republican Party thought him so ignorant, weak, vacillating, and untrustworthy that there was even a move to court-martial him in early 1863. Lincoln felt wretched, saying, "If there's a worse place than hell, I'm in it."[85]

Lincoln was dismayed and depressed and felt utterly alone. Mary, still in mourning for Willie, was unable to offer support. And because her fragile mental

Black soldiers report for duty. Lincoln believed that allowing black soldiers to fight would contribute to restoring the Union.

health made him reluctant to trust her discretion, he was unable to confide in her. He did find some comfort, and probably escape, with Tad and spent as much time with him as possible. A lively, undisciplined nine-year-old boy with a speech impediment that prevented him from conversing with most people, Tad could not read or write or dress himself. This apparent backwardness did not concern Lincoln at all. He felt there would be time later for him to instruct Tad in these basics. Meanwhile, Lincoln indulged the boy more than ever, often allowing him to interrupt cabinet meetings and to curl up and sleep in his office.

Union Troops Still Floundering

By spring 1863 Union troops were floundering and badly needed a victory. General "Fighting Joe" Hooker had replaced Burnside and promised one. He was sent to trap the Confederates at Chancellorsville, Virginia, with seventy thousand men and orders to destroy, not simply defeat, the enemy forces. Victory seemed assured since Union troops outnumbered Confederates two to one. But Hooker was overconfident and would soon join Lincoln's long list of ineffectual generals. He hesitated, and Lee took the offensive and routed the Union troops. Hooker was forced to retreat, giving the Confederates another major victory. Lincoln was a broken man. Having learned from past experience, he had asked to be given the battle plans ahead of time and to be kept informed, and for four days spent most of his time at the War Department, waiting. When he finally received the news, he was extremely distraught. He paced back and forth exclaiming, "My God! My God! What will the country say? What will the country say?"[86]

The weeks following the Union defeat at Chancellorsville were some of the most

As national opposition to Lincoln's policies mounted, the president took comfort in spending time with his young son, Tad.

difficult and depressing for Lincoln. There were more losses at Charleston, in northern Virginia, and in eastern Tennessee. Protests against the war increased, as did the complaints about his incompetence.

THE BATTLE OF GETTYSBURG

The aftermath of the drubbing at Chancellorsville was devastating. After trying to determine what had happened, Lincoln focused his attention on Pennsylvania and on the campaign against Vicksburg, Mississippi, where General Ulysses S. Grant was attempting to take control of the Mississippi River and split the Confederacy in two. Lee had moved north from Virginia and invaded Pennsylvania, and the Army of the Potomac, now under General George Gordon Meade, rushed there to stop Lee. On July 1 the two sides met at Gettysburg in one of the bloodiest battles of the Civil War. In three days, fifty-one thousand troops on both sides were killed, wounded, or captured.

The wait was agonizing for Lincoln. Finally, on July 4 he received news that Union troops had prevailed and Lee had retreated, preventing a Confederate invasion of the North. Also on that morning, Grant triumphed at Vicksburg, taking control of the entire Mississippi River. Lincoln was ecstatic and thought that if Meade would follow through and catch Lee's army, the war would at last be over. But Meade did not catch Lee, and Lincoln was beside himself. "We had them in the hollow of our hand, but we didn't close the hand."[87] Another general

The dead litter the ground at the Battle of Gettysburg, which resulted in the death, injury, or capture of fifty-one thousand troops on both sides.

had failed him. And there was no end in sight to the war.

THE GETTYSBURG ADDRESS

In an attempt to honor those killed, to preserve the Union, and to symbolize the country's purpose, a national cemetery was constructed at Gettysburg on the battlefield where so many had fought and died. Even though Tad was sick and Mary was terrified, having already lost two sons, Lincoln felt he must keep his commitment, so he went to Gettysburg on November 19, 1863, to help dedicate the new cemetery. Inviting the president to speak actually had been an afterthought, but as chief executive of the nation he was asked to "set apart these grounds to their sacred use by a few

appropriate remarks."[88] He followed acclaimed orator Edward Everett, the principal speaker. Everett spoke for two hours, but Lincoln's few words would go down in history. To "a hurricane of applause" and "sobs of smothered emotion,"[89] Lincoln eloquently paid tribute to those who had fought and died there. And he exquisitely made it clear that the goal had become the Union and equality. The war was no longer only to preserve the Union but to create a new nation out of all the spent blood.

FINALLY, A REAL LEADER

Lincoln was still searching for a military leader of courage, tenacity, and genius, the qualities that thus far had allowed Robert E. Lee to triumph repeatedly in the face of overwhelming odds. From the beginning, each Northern general had fallen short. But it looked as though the search would end when General Grant was appointed commander of the western armies the previous September. He was Lincoln's kind of man—unassuming, trustworthy, capable, tenacious, and dedicated—and he accepted Lincoln's policies on emancipation and black recruitment. Most of all, Lincoln liked Grant because "he doesn't worry and bother me. He isn't shrieking for reinforcements all the time. He takes what troops we can safely give him . . . and does the best he can with what he has got."[90] And Grant had basically the same approach to winning the war, no maneuvering, just keep attacking and pounding until the Confederates surrendered. Hoping he could finally bring an end to the war, Lincoln appointed Lieutenant General Grant (the first of that rank since George Washington) to general in chief in March 1864.

Grant planned a rigorous assault on the Confederacy, with several Union armies simultaneously attacking the heartland. General William Tecumseh Sherman would push from Tennessee to take Atlanta, where there was a crucial railway center, then north toward Virginia. Grant would take his troops through the wilderness of Virginia to Richmond. There would be, he promised Lincoln, no turning back. And there was not. During the seven weeks of Grant's Wilderness Campaign, some of the fiercest fighting and heaviest losses of the war were endured.

Lincoln at Gettysburg. His address to the huge crowd became one of the most famous political speeches in history.

ADDRESS DELIVERED AT THE DEDICATION OF THE CEMETERY AT GETTYSBURG NOVEMBER 19, 1863

The Gettysburg Address is considered one of the greatest speeches in the English language. This is the final manuscript, known as the Bliss copy, which Lincoln prepared for Colonel Alexander Bliss to publish in Autographed Leaves of Our Country's Authors *(1864), and is reprinted in* Abraham Lincoln: His Speeches and Writings:

Four score and seven years ago our fathers brought forth on this continent, a new nation, conceived in Liberty, and dedicated to the proposition that all men are created equal.

Now we are engaged in a great civil war, testing whether that nation, or any nation so conceived and so dedicated, can long endure. We are met on a great battlefield of that war. We have come to dedicate a portion of that field, as a final resting place for those who here gave their lives that that nation might live. It is altogether fitting and proper that we should do this.

But, in a larger sense, we can not dedicate—we can not consecrate—we can not hallow—this ground. The brave men, living and dead, who struggled here, have consecrated it, far above our poor power to add or detract. The world will little note, nor long remember what we say here, but it can never forget what they did here. It is for us the living, rather, to be dedicated here to the unfinished work which they who fought here have thus far so nobly advanced. It is rather for us to be here dedicated to the great task remaining before us—that from these honored dead we take increased devotion to that cause for which they gave the last full measure of devotion—that we here highly resolve that these dead shall not have died in vain—that this nation, under God, shall have a new birth of freedom—and that government of the people, by the people, for the people, shall not perish from the earth.

In one week, he lost thirty-two thousand men, but he still pushed forward. By June, Grant was almost to Richmond, but he was stopped at Petersburg by Lee. Grant had advanced only sixty miles, and he had lost sixty thousand men, three times as many as Lee.

"I SHALL NEVER BE GLAD AGAIN"

Throughout the Wilderness Campaign, Lincoln was unable to sleep. He paced the floor in anguish, black rings under his eyes. "My God, my God," he lamented. "Twenty thousand poor souls sent to their final encounter in one day. I cannot bear it. I cannot bear it."[91] He told a friend, "I feel as though I shall never be glad again."[92]

The country, too, was horrified at the losses. By late summer 1864, morale was at its lowest. Both Sherman and Grant were stuck, and there was no end in sight. People blamed Lincoln for all the deaths, and they were pushing for peace talks to settle the war. Democrats called Lincoln the "widow-maker." Many people believed he was inept, uncaring, and a failure, using sometimes contradictory terms like "tyrant," "imbecile," "dazed and utterly foolish," and "weak."

THE NATIONAL UNION PARTY

In the midst of this turmoil, Lincoln had to face the upcoming election. He was committed to proceeding with the election—destined to become the most important one in history—despite the Civil War and the prevailing public opinion. Actually, if the Republican Convention had been held at that time, he probably would not have received the nomination. Fortunately, however, the convention at which the Republican Party selected its ticket for the upcoming national election was held in June, before the terrible losses of the

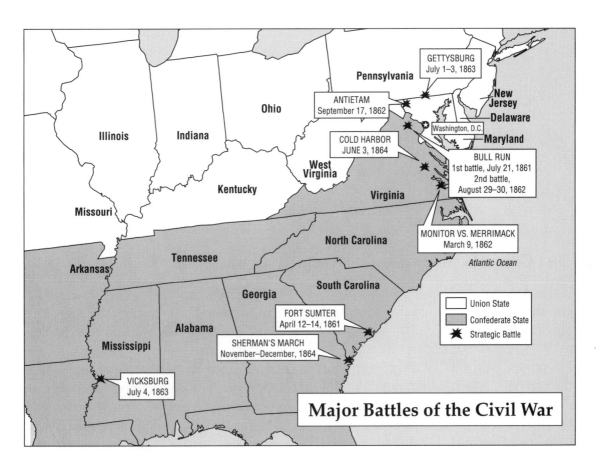

Major Battles of the Civil War

Wilderness Campaign were widely known and sentiment had not turned heavily against the president. Although a majority of Republicans still supported Lincoln, the party was divided. Radicals formed a third party and nominated Frémont. The remaining Republicans, having been joined by pro-war Democrats, renamed the party the National Union Party to emphasize union, to attract more Democrats who supported the war effort, and to disassociate themselves from the radicals. Lincoln was nominated on the first ballot by the National Union Party (which faded away after the 1866 elections), and Andrew Johnson, a Democrat, was nominated for vice president. Lincoln truly wanted to win:

> I confess I desire to be reelected. God knows I do not want the labor and responsibility of the office for another four years. But I honestly believe I can better serve the nation in its need and peril than any new man could possibly do. I want to finish this job.[93]

"I'm Going to be Beaten"

But that summer it looked as though others did not want him to win. Because of repeated losses on the battlefield and diminished public support, many, including Lincoln himself, felt certain he would lose the election. Pessimistic members of his own party even tried to replace him as the nominee. On August 23 Lincoln said, "This morning, as for some days past, it seems exceedingly possible that this administration will not be reelected. I'm going to be beaten. And unless some great change takes place, badly."[94] As had been anticipated, on August 29 the Democrats nominated General George B. McClellan, ever a thorn in Lincoln's side.

The Beginning of the End

As luck, or Providence, would have it, a great change did take place. On September 2, Lincoln received a dispatch from Sherman: "So Atlanta is ours and fairly won. . . ."[95] This victory changed everything. It was the beginning of the end for the Confederacy, and it almost surely changed the minds of many voters who had hated the president the month before. Sherman destroyed army depots, factories, and warehouses, reducing to rubble anything that could help the military. Then he began his devastating march to the sea, destroying everything in his path. Meanwhile, Grant was closing in on Richmond.

Election Day

Election Day on November 8 was gray and raining. Lincoln spent the day alone at the White House. About 7 P.M., he ventured out into the heavy rain and across the grounds to the War Department telegraph office to check the election results. Because of the heavy storm, the telegraph wires were not working well and results were slow coming in. By midnight, it was apparent that Lincoln had won. He was relieved it was finally over. When he left the War Office about 2 A.M. the rain had stopped. He was greeted by serenaders with a brass band, cheering and calling for a speech. He told them:

> I earnestly believe that the consequences of this day's work, if it be as you assure me and as now seems probable, will be to the lasting advantage, if not to the very salvation, of the country. . . . I do not impugn the

Lincoln did not believe he would be reelected, but when it became apparent that the Union was winning the war, renewed voter support kept him in office.

motives of any one opposed to me. It is no pleasure to me to triumph over any one; but I give thanks to the Almighty for this evidence of the people's resolution to stand by free government and the rights of humanity.[96]

Lincoln received 55 percent of the popular vote to McClellan's 45 percent, and he won 212 of 233 electoral votes, securing his reelection and beginning the fateful countdown.

THE THIRTEENTH AMENDMENT

After the election and the vindication that resulted from the long-awaited military victories, Lincoln enjoyed widespread support in Congress, even from former opponents. He capitalized on this assistance and the powers of his office to persuade Democrats to support the proposed constitutional amendment to abolish slavery everywhere in the United States. Lincoln was passionate and adamant about it, earlier having convinced the National Union Party to include the amendment as a plank in their platform. He was convinced that this measure would do away with the original cause of the rebellion and eliminate any questions about the legality or permanence of the Emancipation Proclamation. The amendment had failed to pass in the previous session of Congress, but with his urging, more than the required two-thirds of the House members voted for it on the final ballot. On January 31, 1865, the House passed the Thirteenth

AFTER THE THIRTEENTH AMENDMENT

Lincoln knew that to guarantee the abolishment of slavery there would have to be a constitutional amendment following the Emancipation Proclamation, which demonstrated the federal government's opposition to slavery, but was in fact simply a war powers act executed as commander in chief. He worked tirelessly, using his political skill and influence to achieve this, and the Thirteenth Amendment to the Constitution was passed by the Senate on April 8, 1864, by the House of Representatives on January 31, 1985, and finally ratified (by three-fourths of the states, as required by the Constitution) on December 5, 1865, eight months after Lincoln was assassinated.

But as Lincoln pondered what would become of the slaves once they were free, he realized that emancipation alone would not be sufficient, and as early as 1864 he advocated universal suffrage (for black men).

After emancipation, many former slaves still labored in conditions that were much the same as before the war. Moreover, state legislatures of governors appointed by the new president, Andrew Johnson, were proslavery and passed laws designed to keep blacks in poverty and servitude. Frederick Douglass and the American Anti-Slavery Society joined radical Republicans, led by antislavery senators Charles Sumner and Thaddeus Stevens, to campaign for voting rights for black men. In 1866, over the veto of President Johnson, Congress passed the Civil Rights Act, which granted citizenship to native-born Americans (except Indians). Congress also passed the Fourteenth Amendment, ratified in 1868, which granted equal protection under the law to blacks, but still did not guarantee them the right to vote. Finally, 1868 saw the proposal of the Fifteenth Amendment, guaranteeing all citizens—regardless of race—the right to vote. It was ratified in 1870.

Between 1868 and 1870, the Southern states were readmitted to the United States, and a number of blacks were elected to Congress and the state legislatures. But it would not be until a century later that blacks' voting rights were truly protected and guaranteed: the Civil Rights Act in 1960, reaffirms voting rights for all American citizens; the Twenty-fourth Amendment, ratified in 1964, outlaws poll taxes for national elections; and the Voting Rights Act of 1965 nullifies local laws and practices (chiefly used against minorities) that prevent qualified registered voters from voting.

Amendment and submitted it to the states for ratification. It was, for Lincoln, a "great moral victory" and the culmination of his goal and his destiny to abolish slavery, but he would not live to see its ratification.

Chapter

9 Destiny

Inauguration Day on March 4, 1865, was another cold, rainy day. But as Lincoln began to deliver his second inaugural address, the sun, as if to highlight his words, burst through the clouds. It was an eloquent speech, intended to explain the pain and suffering of the past four years. First, he recalled how the war had started:

> On the occasion corresponding to this four years ago, all thoughts were anxiously directed to an impending civil war. All dreaded it—all sought to avert it. . . . Both parties deprecated war; but one of them would *make* war rather than let the nation survive; and the other would *accept* war rather than let it perish.

Later, he contemplated why the war continued—perhaps as punishment for allowing slavery to exist:

> If we shall suppose that American Slavery is one of those offences which, in the providence of God, must needs come, but which, having continued through His appointed time, He now wills to remove, and that He gives to both North and South, this terrible war, as the woe

due to those by whom the offence came. . . . Fondly do we hope—fervently do we pray—that this mighty Scourge of war will speedily pass away.

And it was supposed to heal, to unify. Carefully, he tried to lift the burden, the responsibility, the guilt off the shoulders of both the North and the South. Neither was to blame. It was God's will. He closed with:

> With malice toward none; with charity for all; with firmness in the right, as God gives us to see the right, let us strive on to finish the work we are in; to bind up the nation's wounds; to care for him who shall have borne the battle, and for his widow, and his orphan—to do all which may achieve and cherish a just and lasting peace, among ourselves, and with all nations.[97]

CLOSING IN ON VICTORY

Meanwhile the Union army was continuing its march to victory. Sherman had

Lincoln's second inauguration took place on March 4, 1865. Speaking at the ceremony, the president eloquently spoke of healing the division between North and South.

captured the coastal city of Savannah, Georgia, on December 20, offering it as a Christmas gift in a message to Lincoln. He headed north, burning homes, destroying property, confiscating or setting free livestock. After the fall of Atlanta, Sherman changed the nature of the war. It became total war, causing suffering for everyone—soldiers and civilians, young and old. Charleston, South Carolina, surrendered in February, and by March, Sherman had stormed through North Carolina on his way to Virginia, where his troops would join Grant's.

On March 23, Lincoln, along with Mary, Tad, Mary's maid, and a White House guard, started down the Potomac on the *River Queen* to Grant's headquarters. The reason for the trip was twofold. Rest and relaxation for the president—he

had been so exhausted after the inauguration, he had to spend a few days in bed. The four years of war were showing. The lines and furrows on his face had deepened, his cheeks were sunken. He had lost a lot of weight and was extremely thin. Although he was fifty-six, he looked much older. He was tired and tortured.

DOWN THE RIVER

Once Lincoln was away from Washington, he felt better. But Mary, who was fragile emotionally, did not. She made a scene by publicly criticizing Lincoln and unjustly and irrationally accusing the young, pretty wife of one of the officers of flirting with him, then demanding that

"WITH MALICE TOWARD NONE"

General William Tecumseh Sherman joined General Ulysses Grant for his meeting with President Lincoln on the River Queen *from March 27 to 28, 1865, where according to Sherman in his* Memoirs, *Lincoln made it clear he wanted the war to end with no punishment or retaliation toward the rebels. Sherman wrote:*

I know, when I left him, that I was more than ever impressed by his kindly nature, his deep and earnest sympathy with the afflictions of the whole people, resulting from the war, and by the march of hostile armies through the South; and that his earnest desire seemed to be to end the war speedily, without more bloodshed or devastation, and to restore all the men of both sections to their homes. In the language of his second inaugural address, he seemed to have "charity for all, malice toward none," and above all, an absolute faith in the courage, manliness, and integrity of the armies in the field. When at rest or listening, his legs and arms seemed to hang almost lifeless, and his face was care-worn and haggard; but, the moment he began to talk, his face lightened up, his tall form, as it were, unfolded, and he was the very impersonation of good humor and fellowship. The last words I recall as addressed to me were that he would feel better when I was back at Goldsboro. We parted at the gangway of the *River Queen*, about noon of March 28, and I never saw him again. Of all the men I ever met, he seemed to possess more of the elements of greatness, combined with goodness, than any other.

Lincoln relieve the officer of his command. To the embarrassment of everyone, particularly Lincoln, Mary continued her tantrum when the presidential party returned to the *River Queen*. Lincoln bore it silently and stoically until she tore into him when he spoke to her, and he walked quietly away, without giving voice to his pain and humiliation. Mary stayed in her cabin for three days, and then Lincoln sent her home to Washington, explaining that she was not feeling well.

VISITING THE FIELD

Lincoln also met with Grant and Sherman and ordered them not to let the rebels get away. It had happened so many times in the past and Lincoln could not bear to go through—or have the country go through—that again. And he wanted them to offer generous terms of surrender. He did not want any more bloodshed, and he did not want anybody punished. He just wanted the defeated Confederate soldiers to return to their homes and families and to continue their lives peacefully, rejoining the Union.

Lincoln visited the commanders and reviewed the troops. He also visited a field hospital, where he stayed for five hours, greeting, shaking hands, cheering up the ill and wounded. While there, he made a point of visiting the hospitalized Confederates. He stopped at the bed of a wounded rebel and asked him whether he would shake his hand if he knew he was President Lincoln. The young soldier looked up at him with tears in his eyes, and Lincoln, looking back with tear-filled eyes, took his hand and shook it.

THE FALL OF RICHMOND

On April 2 Petersburg, Virginia, fell, with the mayor surrendering the city and Lee informing Jefferson Davis that he must flee Richmond. That night, the Confederate government evacuated Richmond and set fire to the warehouses and bridges, leaving its capital burning. The following day it was occupied by the Union, while Lee's demoralized army was chased by determined Union troops. It was clear that the end of the war was near.

On April 4 Lincoln, along with Tad, was taken into Richmond where he viewed the ruins firsthand. Some freed slaves recognized him and ran over to him saying, "Bless the Lord, there is the great Messiah! . . . Glory Hallelujah!"[98] When they knelt and tried to kiss his feet, he told them they should only kneel to God and give thanks to Him for their freedom.

Wanting to visit what had been the seat of the rebel government, Lincoln went to Jefferson Davis's headquarters, the abandoned Confederate White House, and went to Davis's office where, to the cheers of his Union escorts, he sat in his chair.

LEE SURRENDERS AT APPOMATTOX

A few days later, on April 9, General Robert E. Lee surrendered to General Ulysses S. Grant at Appomattox Courthouse in Virginia. After four years, the war was finally over. More than six hundred thousand had given their lives—more than the total death toll for all U.S. wars from the Revolution to the Korean War combined.

Lincoln was informed of the surrender that night, and at daylight ordered the firing of five hundred cannons. A crowd gathered at the White House, calling for the president. He spoke briefly and told them he would prepare a speech for the next night, for a formal celebration. Then he had the band play "Dixie," commenting that the Confederate anthem was "one of the best tunes I have ever heard."[99]

LINCOLN'S LAST PUBLIC ADDRESS

The following evening, Lincoln gave what would be his last public address. The crowd was enormous and jubilant. They had come to celebrate and revel in the victory. And they wanted to hear their president recount it for them. After repeated calls, cheers, and applause, Lincoln finally

General Robert E. Lee (seated left) surrenders to General Ulysses S. Grant (seated center) at Appomattox Courthouse. A war in which 600,000 had died was over at last.

appeared and began to read his carefully prepared speech, "We meet this evening, not in sorrow, but in gladness of heart. The evacuation of Petersburg and Richmond, and the surrender of the principal insurgent army, give hope of a righteous and speedy peace whose joyous expression can not be restrained."[100]

Lincoln went on to thank God and General Grant and to talk about reuniting and rebuilding, rather than celebration. In this vein, much of the speech was about the reconstructed government of Louisiana and its relationship to the Union. He pointed out that it was unsatisfactory that Louisiana was denying suffrage to blacks. And he took that opportunity to mention publicly for the first time the extension of suffrage to blacks, making known his wish that black

veterans, especially, be allowed to vote. It was probably this appeal that convinced John Wilkes Booth to carry out his plan to assassinate Lincoln.

ASSASSINATION FEARS AND THREATS

There had been threats before—since before the election of 1860, in fact. At first, they troubled him. As president-elect, he had followed his advisors' suggestion that he sneak into Washington in disguise, an act he always regretted. The threats drove Mary to distraction, and early on she expressed the fear that her husband would meet a violent end. That fear was always with her, increasing as time passed.

Once Lincoln was in the White House, the threats no longer bothered him, and he essentially ignored them, instructing his secretaries to throw the letters away before he saw them. He believed that in a democracy the president could not be shielded or hidden from the public. Lincoln understood it would be impossible to be completely protected, and perhaps his fatalism entered in when he said, "It would never do for a president to have guards with drawn sabres at his door, as if he fancied he were, or were trying to be, an emperor."[101] And further, if a group of conspirators plotted his death, "no vigilance could keep them out. . . . A conspiracy to assassinate, if such there were, could easily obtain a pass to see me for any one or more of its instruments."[102]

With Lincoln's reelection, as hostility toward him increased, so did threats to assassinate or kidnap him. Anti-Lincoln Confederates favored kidnapping, believing if Lincoln were whisked away to Richmond, he would be forced to negotiate with the Confederate government.

In July 1863, when Mary suffered a fall from her carriage on the way back to the White House from the Soldiers' Home, it was believed that someone had loosened the bolt securing the seat in an attempt to assassinate Lincoln. And in late September 1864, when Lincoln was returning to the Soldiers' Home, someone fired a shot at him, scaring his horse and causing it to bolt. The next day, the president's hat was found with a bullet hole through the crown.

JOHN WILKES BOOTH

John Wilkes Booth was not the first to try to kill Abraham Lincoln, but he was probably the most impassioned. Booth, an actor renowned for his good looks, was actually a Northerner, but his sympathy was with the Confederacy. He was a racist and, by his family's admission, emotionally unstable. Booth believed that "this country was formed for the *white*, not for the black man" and he considered slavery "one of the greatest blessings (both for themselves and for us) that God ever bestowed upon a favored nation."[103]

Originally, Booth had planned to kidnap Lincoln, take him to Richmond, and exchange him for Confederate prisoners of war. He had even enlisted some friends for the help he would need. When changes in Lincoln's plans—and Lee's surrender—spoiled his abduction schemes, Booth began to contemplate assassination. And when, on April 11, he heard Lincoln advocate suffrage for blacks, that, to him, meant the ruin of the country, and

John Wilkes Booth's racism undoubtedly fueled his decision to kill Lincoln.

he vowed, "That is the last speech he will ever make."[104]

GOOD FRIDAY

On April 14, 1865, there was an announcement in the newspaper that the president, accompanied by the victorious General Grant, would be attending a play called *Our American Cousin* at Ford's Theater that night. Despite his advisors' warning him and his bodyguard's imploring him not to go, Lincoln was determined to see the play. He was tired of the frequent warnings, and an evening at the theater had become one of his few forms of relaxation.

Earlier that day, Lincoln and Mary had taken a carriage ride and had, for the first time in a long time, enjoyed themselves. Lincoln's spirits were high. He commented that they must be more cheerful in the future, that the war and the loss of Willie had made them miserable. It was Good Friday; Easter was two days away. Mary was buoyed by her husband's good mood, as Booth must have been by his own good luck.

Lincoln would be accessible, and accompanied by his general. A well-known actor, Booth could move freely about a theater without arousing suspicion. Unbeknownst to Booth, the guard outside the presidential box would leave his post and go downstairs to watch the play.

"NOW HE BELONGS TO THE AGES"

At 10:13 P.M., Booth quietly entered the presidential box and standing about two

A Bodyguard's Story

William H. Crook was a presidential bodyguard. He started as a plainclothes police officer assigned to guard the president from 4 P.M. to midnight. Then his shift changed to midnight to 8 A.M. where he was seated outside Lincoln's bedroom to guard him while he slept. Finally he was promoted to daytime duty. He reported directly to the president.

In 1911 Crook published a memoir of his White House experiences, edited and interviewed by Henry Rood. It offers an interesting up close view from an unusual perspective. This excerpt is from that memoir, as quoted in Lincoln: As I Knew Him:

The only time that President Lincoln failed to say good-night to me—when we parted after having been together for hours—was on the evening shortly before he started for Ford's Theater, where he was murdered. As I mentioned on another occasion, some years ago, Mr. Lincoln had told me that afternoon of a dream he had had for three succesive nights, concerning his impending assassination. Of course, the constant dread of such a calamity made me somewhat nervous, and I almost begged him to remain in the Executive Mansion that night, and not to go to the theater. But he would not disappoint Mrs. Lincoln and others who were to be present. Then I urged that he allow me to stay on duty and accompany him; but he would not hear of this either.

"No, Crook," he said kindly but firmly, "you have had a long, hard day's work already, and must go home to sleep and rest. I cannot afford to have you get all tired out and exhausted."

It was then that he neglected, for the first and only time, to say good-night to me. Instead, he turned, with his kind, grave face and said: "Good-bye, Crook," and went into his room.

I thought of it at the moment; and a few hours later, when the awful news flashed over Washington that he had been shot, his last words were so burned into my memory that they never have been forgotten, and never can be forgotten.

feet away, shot Lincoln in the head. Booth quickly jumped from the box onto the stage, breaking his leg and yelling, *"Sic semper tyrannis"* ("Thus always to tyrants"—also the Virginia state motto). As he limped away, some spectators, recognizing him, wondered whether the spectacle was part of the play.

Lincoln never regained consciousness. He was taken across the street to a boarding house and laid diagonally, because of his height, across a poster bed. Mary, hysterical and inconsolable, remained at his side. Lincoln's son Robert, members of the cabinet, congressmen, and other officials filled the room. At 7:22 A.M., April 15,

Abraham Lincoln died. Secretary of War Edwin M. Stanton, who had persistently criticized the president, spoke for all when he said, "Now he belongs to the ages."[105]

Booth escaped on a horse that was saddled and waiting outside the theater. He was caught by federal troops and shot in a barn in Virginia twelve days later. He had written in his diary that the country owed all its troubles to Lincoln "and God simply made me the instrument of his punishment."[106] Though he was successful in assassinating Lincoln, his scheme to give the Confederacy one last chance by destabilizing the U.S. government failed. Grant, having changed his mind at the last minute, was not at the theater.

LAID TO REST

Lincoln's funeral was on April 19 in the East Room of the White House, after which a detachment of black troops led a funeral procession to the Capitol where the dead president would lie in state for two days while thousands of mourners waited in the rain to pay their final respects. The train that carried Lincoln's remains to Springfield for burial followed the same route the man had taken when he first came to Washington as president-elect. The procession made stops along the way to allow a grieving nation to pay tribute.

As the funeral train slowly pulled into Springfield on May 3, it was met by tens

An illustration depicts John Wilkes Booth shooting Lincoln. Mortally wounded, the president died the next day.

MARY TODD LINCOLN

Mary Todd Lincoln was holding Abraham Lincoln's hand when John Wilkes Booth assassinated him. She never recovered from the shock and in 1875 was declared insane and committed to a private sanitarium.

Most experts agree that today she would probably be diagnosed as schizophrenic. Her life had been filled with tragedy, each catastrophe pushing her closer to mental breakdown, and her husband's assassination was more than she could bear.

Even though Mary Todd Lincoln achieved her goal—she married a president, and she adored him—her life was not a happy one. Throughout her marriage, her personality was unstable, and she became increasingly erratic, fearful, and insecure. She was devastated by the deaths of four-year-old Eddie in 1850 and eleven-year-old Willie in 1862. She was so distraught when Willie, her favorite child, died that

Lincoln warned her she would end up in an asylum if she did not get a hold of herself. In 1871 eighteen-year-old Tad died of tuberculosis, worsening her fragile mental condition. Robert, her remaining son, had her committed in 1875. She was released after about four months to the custody of her sister, Elizabeth Edwards, in Springfield.

Mary Todd Lincoln lived for six more years in ill health, wandering from city to city. She returned to her sister's care in Springfield in 1882 and died on July 15.

Always mentally fragile, Mary Todd Lincoln never recovered from her husband's death.

of thousands of people waiting and mourning. A military band played a funeral dirge while guns fired a salute and all the bells in Springfield tolled. Lincoln was laid to rest at Oak Ridge Cemetery beside his sons Eddie and Willie.

The Most Important Election in U.S. History

The election of 1864 is considered the most important election in U.S. history and is an essential part of Lincoln's legacy. Its impact still reverberates today for many reasons. First, it is miraculous that the election was even held in the midst of a civil war. This exemplifies how fundamental the democratic process is to this country. It truly is the foundation on which all else is built. Lincoln knew this and understood how important it was to keep that foundation firmly in place. He never considered suspending or postponing the election. This disciplined adherence to democratic principles is especially remarkable because to many, including

Lincoln is pictured near Sharpsburg, Maryland, a few weeks after the Battle of Antietam. Even though the nation was locked in a civil war and his own popularity was in steep decline, Lincoln never considered not holding the 1864 presidential election.

Lincoln himself, losing had looked like a certainty. In fact, even his nomination as his party's candidate was in doubt—and widely opposed.

Lincoln's courage, strength, and faith in the constitutional system reflected his belief that the right to vote is essential to democratic government and a civil act so basic that nothing, even civil war, can be allowed to interfere with a scheduled election. Further, the right to vote was reinforced by allowing absentee voting by soldiers for the first time. And the election established that democratic government prevails over all other rights of the individual or the nation.

Never before had U.S. citizens been given the opportunity to vote on the issue of slavery. In 1864 that issue was before them, and they voted against it. The election constituted popular ratification of the Emancipation Proclamation. (The slaves not covered by that document were freed some eight months after Lincoln's death with the ratification of the Thirteenth Amendment, thereby ending slavery in the Western world.) This remains one of the most important events of all time. Lincoln was correct (though modest) when he predicted, "If my name ever goes into history, it will be for this act."[107]

Notes

Introduction: "The Struggle Should Be Maintained"

1. Quoted in David E. Long, *The Jewel of Liberty: Abraham's Re-election and the End of Slavery*. Mechanicsburg, PA: Stackpole Books, 1994, p. xvi.

Chapter 1: A Simple, Poor Beginning

2. Quoted in David Herbert Donald, *Lincoln*. New York: Simon & Schuster, 1995, p. 19.
3. Quoted in Mark E. Neely Jr., *The Last Best Hope of Earth: Abraham Lincoln and the Promise of America*. Cambridge, MA: Harvard University Press, 1993, p. 36.
4. Roy P. Basler, ed., *Abraham Lincoln: His Speeches and Writings*. Cleveland: Da Capo Press, 1946, p. 548.
5. Quoted in Donald, *Lincoln*, p. 28.
6. Quoted in Harold Holzer, ed., *Lincoln As I Knew Him*. Chapel Hill, NC: Algonquin Books, 1999, pp. 14–17.
7. Quoted in Carl Sandburg, *Abraham Lincoln: The Prairie Years and The War Years*. New York: Harcourt, Brace, 1954, p. 13.
8. Donald, *Lincoln*, p. 32.
9. Quoted in Donald, *Lincoln*, p. 32.
10. Basler, *Abraham Lincoln*, p. 547.
11. Basler, *Abraham Lincoln*, p. 511.

Chapter 2: Entering Politics

12. Quoted in Donald, *Lincoln*, p. 40.
13. Basler, *Abraham Lincoln*, p. 57.
14. Quoted in Donald, *Lincoln*, p. 44.
15. Basler, *Abraham Lincoln*, p. 551.
16. Quoted in Douglas L. Wilson, *Honor's Voice: The Transformation of Abraham Lincoln*. New York: Alfred A. Knopf, 1998, p. 90.
17. Quoted in Wilson, *Honor's Voice*, p. 104.
18. Quoted in Wilson, *Honor's Voice*, pp. 165–166.

Chapter 3: From Springfield to Washington

19. Basler, *Abraham Lincoln*, p. 81.
20. Wilson, *Honor's Voice*, p. 181.
21. Quoted in Wilson, *Honor's Voice*, p. 187.
22. Wilson, *Honor's Voice*, p. 193.
23. Quoted in Wilson, *Honor's Voice*, p. 189.
24. Quoted in Donald, *Lincoln*, p. 354.
25. Quoted in Wilson, *Honor's Voice*, p. 309.
26. Quoted in Wilson, *Honor's Voice*, p. 236.
27. Quoted in *Lincoln*, produced and directed by Peter W. Kunhardt, written and produced by Phillip B. Kunhardt III and Phillip B. Kunhardt Jr., narrated by James Earl Jones. ABC, 12/26, 12/27/1992.

Chapter 4: A Roundabout Route to the Presidency

28. Quoted in Holzer, *Lincoln: As I Knew Him*, p. 62.
29. Quoted in Holzer, *Lincoln: As I Knew Him*, p. 77.
30. Basler, *Abraham Lincoln*, p. 554.
31. Basler, *Abraham Lincoln*, pp. 303–304.
32. Quoted in Donald, *Lincoln*, p. 176.
33. Quoted in Donald, *Lincoln*, p. 166.
34. Mario M. Cuomo and Harold Holzer, *Lincoln On Democracy*. New York: HarperCollins, 1990, p. 57.
35. Quoted in Donald, *Lincoln*, p. 192.
36. Quoted in Donald, *Lincoln*, p. 191.

37. Quoted in Donald, *Lincoln*, p. 192.

38. Quoted in Cuomo and Holzer, *Lincoln On Democracy*, p. 135.

Chapter 5: For the Union

39. Quoted in Donald, *Lincoln*, p. 269.

40. Basler, *Abraham Lincoln*, p. 588.

41. Basler, *Abraham Lincoln*, p. 580.

42. Basler, *Abraham Lincoln*, p. 582.

43. Basler, *Abraham Lincoln*, p. 588.

44. Philip Shaw Paludan, *The Presidency of Abraham Lincoln*. Lawrence, KS: University Press of Kansas, 1994, p. 77.

45. Paludan, *The Presidency of Abraham Lincoln*, p. 80.

46. Basler, *Abraham Lincoln*, p. 600.

47. Paludan, *The Presidency of Abraham Lincoln*, p. 80.

Chapter 6: Commander in Chief

48. Quoted in Holzer, *Lincoln: As I Knew Him*, p. 134.

49. Quoted in Donald, *Lincoln*, p. 334.

50. Quoted in *Abraham and Mary Lincoln: A House Divided*, produced and directed by David Grubin, written by David Grubin and Geoffrey C. Ward, narrated by David McCullough. PBS (The American Experience), 2/19, 2/20, 2/21/2001.

51. Quoted in *Abraham and Mary Lincoln* (PBS).

52. Quoted in Donald, *Lincoln*, p. 337.

53. Quoted in *Lincoln* (ABC).

54. Quoted in Holzer, *Lincoln: As I Knew Him*, p. 149.

55. Quoted in Holzer, *Lincoln: As I Knew Him*, p. 160.

56. Quoted in Paludan, *The Presidency of Abraham Lincoln*, p. 120.

57. Quoted in Donald, *Lincoln*, p. 349.

58. Quoted in Donald, *Lincoln*, p. 349.

59. Quoted in *Abraham and Mary Lincoln* (PBS).

60. Quoted in *Abraham and Mary Lincoln* (PBS).

61. Quoted in Neely, *The Last Best Hope of Earth*, p. 94.

Chapter 7: The Great Emancipator

62. Quoted in Wilson, *Honor's Voice*, p. 166.

63. Quoted in John Hope Franklin, *The Emancipation Proclamation*. New York: Doubleday, 1963, p. 25.

64. Quoted in Donald, *Lincoln*, p. 363.

65. Quoted in Donald, *Lincoln*, p. 365.

66. Donald, *Lincoln*, p. 364.

67. Quoted in Franklin, *The Emancipation Proclamation*, p. 50.

68. Quoted in Donald, *Lincoln*, p. 366.

69. Quoted in *Lincoln* (ABC).

70. Quoted in Donald, *Lincoln*, p. 527.

71. Quoted in Holzer, *Lincoln: As I Knew Him*, pp. 208–210.

72. Quoted in Donald, *Lincoln*, p. 371.

73. Quoted in Donald, *Lincoln*, p. 374.

74. Quoted in Franklin, *The Emancipation Proclamation*, p. 50.

75. Quoted in Franklin, *The Emancipation Proclamation*, p. 62.

76. Paludan, *The Presidency of Abraham Lincoln*, p. 155.

77. Quoted in Franklin, *The Emancipation Proclamation*, p. 67.

78. Quoted in Franklin, *The Emancipation Proclamation*, p. 68.

79. Quoted in *Abraham and Mary Lincoln* (PBS).

80. Quoted in *Abraham and Mary Lincoln* (PBS).

81. Quoted in Sandburg, *Abraham Lincoln*, p. 344.

82. Quoted in Cuomo and Holzer, *Lincoln On Democracy*, p. 270.

83. Quoted in Sandburg, *Abraham Lincoln*, p. 270.

Chapter 8: Countdown to Destiny

84. Quoted in Donald, *Lincoln*, p. 431.

85. Quoted in *Abraham and Mary Lincoln* (PBS).

86. Quoted in Donald, *Lincoln*, p. 436.

87. Quoted in *Abraham and Mary Lincoln* (PBS).

88. Quoted in Sandburg, *Abraham Lincoln*, p. 439.

89. Quoted in Cuomo and Holzer, *Lincoln On Democacy*, p. 307.

90. Quoted in Donald, *Lincoln*, p. 497.

91. Quoted in *Lincoln* (ABC).

92. Quoted in *Abraham and Mary Lincoln* (PBS).

93. Quoted in *Lincoln* (ABC).

94. Quoted in *Lincoln* (ABC).

95. Quoted in Sandburg, *Abraham Lincoln*, p. 549.

96. Quoted in Sandburg, *Abraham Lincoln*, p. 611.

Chapter 9: Destiny

97. Basler, *Abraham Lincoln*, p. 793.

98. Quoted in Donald, *Lincoln*, p. 576.

99. Quoted in Donald, *Lincoln*, p. 581.

100. Basler, *Abraham Lincoln*, p. 796.

101. Quoted in Donald, *Lincoln*, p. 547.

102. Quoted in Donald, *Lincoln*, p. 548.

103. Quoted in Neely, *The Last Best Hope of Earth*, p. 190.

104. Quoted in Donald, *Lincoln*, p. 588.

105. Quoted in Donald, *Lincoln*, p. 599.

106. Quoted in Donald, *Lincoln*, p. 597.

Epilogue: The Most Important Election in U.S. History

107. Quoted in Cuomo and Holzer, *Lincoln On Democacy*, p. 270.

For Further Reading

Books

Thomas Bracken, *Abraham Lincoln* (Overcoming Adversity). Philadelphia: Chelsea House Publishers, 1998. This book, part of a series on overcoming adversity, focuses on how Lincoln faced personal tragedies and difficulties and national problems.

Roger Bruns, *Abraham Lincoln* (World Leaders Past & Present). New York: Chelsea House Publishers, 1986. This book, part of a series on world leaders, emphasizes the qualities and situations that helped to make Lincoln such a successful and celebrated leader.

Russell Freedman, *Lincoln: A Photobiography*. New York: Clarion Books, 1987. A well-written, informative biography, with many good photographs and some drawings and cartoons.

Sterling North, *Abe Lincoln: Log Cabin to White House*. New York: Random House, 1956. A biography that focuses on Lincoln's childhood and youth on the frontier and follows his rise to the presidency.

Websites

The Abraham Lincoln Association (www.alincolnassoc.com). The Abraham Lincoln Association was organized in 1908 as the Lincoln Centennial Association.

Abraham Lincoln Online (http://showcase.netins.net/web/creative/lincoln.html). A comprehensive site that includes links for students, with speeches, books, places, news, searches, and discussion.

Lincoln/Net (http://lincoln.lib.niu.edu). Lincoln/Net presents historical materials from Abraham Lincoln's Illinois years (1830–1861), including Lincoln's writings and speeches, as well as other materials illuminating antebellum Illinois.

Mr. Lincoln's Virtual Library (http://memory.loc.gov). Mr. Lincoln's Virtual Library highlights two collections at the Library of Congress that illuminate the life of Abraham Lincoln (1809–1865): The Abraham Lincoln (approximately twenty thousand items including correspondence and papers accumulated primarily during Lincoln's presidency) and the "We'll Sing to Abe Our Song!" online collection. Mr. Lincoln's Virtual Library provides access to a variety of documents and resources about Abraham Lincoln.

The Time of the Lincolns (www.pbs.org/wgbh). A companion to the film *Abraham and Mary Lincoln: A House Divided* (The American Experience/PBS). Site includes Map, Foot Soldiers (follow soldiers into war), Virtual Tour (slave cabin and conditions of slavery); Partisan Politics, Slavery & Freedom, A Rising Nation, Americans at War, and A Woman's World.

The History Channel (www.thehistorychannel.com). A wealth of information on everything historical with searches available by topic, period, name, etc.

Works Consulted

Books

Roy P. Basler, ed., *Abraham Lincoln: His Speeches and Writings.* Cleveland: Da Capo Press, Inc., 1946. Lincoln's speeches and writings with critical and analytical notes by Roy P. Basler and a preface by Carl Sandburg.

LaWanda Cox, *Lincoln and Black Freedom: A Study in Presidential Leadership.* Columbia, SC: University of South Carolina Press, 1981. An examination of Lincoln as he related to emancipation and black freedom and equality, in the context of his time.

Mario M. Cuomo and Harold Holzer, *Lincoln On Democracy.* New York: HarperCollins, 1990. An outstanding collection of Lincoln's words on democracy, freedom, and equality, with enlightening and informative essays by leading historians and an enlightening preface by former New York Governor Mario Cuomo and an excellent introduction by historian Harold Holzer.

David Herbert Donald, *Lincoln.* New York: Simon & Schuster, 1995. A critically acclaimed and extensively researched and documented biography. The author, a professor emeritus at Harvard, has twice won the Pulitzer Prize for biography and has written numerous books on Lincoln and the Civil War.

Don E. Fehrenbacher, ed., *Lincoln: Speeches and Writings 1832–1858 (Speeches, Letters, and Miscellaneous Writings, The Lincoln-Douglas Debates).* New York: Penguin Books, 1989. Lincoln's speeches and letters plus other writings and the Lincoln-Douglas debates with notes by Don E. Fehrenbacher.

John Hope Franklin, *The Emancipation Proclamation.* New York: Doubleday, 1963. A detailed evaluation of the evolution of the Emancipation Proclamation and its significance in U.S. history.

Harold Holzer, ed., *Lincoln: As I Knew Him.* Chapel Hill, NC: Algonquin Books, 1999. A collection of diary entries, letters, book excerpts, and speeches written by people who actually met or knew Lincoln—friends, enemies, acquaintances, coworkers, etc.—a good cross-section offering interesting insights.

David E. Long, *The Jewel of Liberty: Abraham Lincoln's Re-election and the End of Slavery.* Mechanicsburg, PA: Stackpole Books, 1994. Long systematically makes the case that the presidential election of 1864 was the most important one in history.

Mark E. Neely Jr., *The Fate of Liberty: Abraham Lincoln and Civil Liberties.* New

York: Oxford University Press, 1991. Winner of the 1992 Pulitzer Prize in History, this book gives a detailed analysis and insights into Lincoln's policies pertaining to civil rights.

Mark E. Neely Jr., *The Last Best Hope of Earth: Abraham Lincoln and the Promise of America.* Cambridge, MA: Harvard University Press, 1993. This book focuses on the period between summer 1860 and spring 1865, Lincoln's presidency, emphasizing his political life.

Phillip Shaw Paludan, *The Presidency of Abraham Lincoln.* Lawrence, KS: University Press of Kansas, 1994. An insightful study of Lincoln's presidency, while the nation was at war, by a history professor and authority on the Civil War.

Robert Hunt Rhodes, ed., *All For the Union: The Civil War Diary and Letters of Elisha Hunt Rhodes.* New York: Orion Books, 1985. Detailed, fascinating, first-hand account of Elisha Hunt Rhodes, who participated in every battle of the Civil War.

Carl Sandburg, *Abraham Lincoln: The Prairie Years and The War Years.* New York: Harcourt, Brace, 1954. Distilled by Sandburg from his six-volume biography (called "the greatest historical biography of our generation"), considered the standard, with new material added.

Gary Wills, *Lincoln at Gettysburg: The Words That Remade America.* New York: Simon & Schuster, 1992. Professor and historian Wills examines the Gettysburg Address and analyzes its origins as well as its meaning, both when it was written and today.

Douglas L. Wilson, *Honor's Voice: The Transformation of Abraham Lincoln.* New York: Alfred A. Knopf, 1998. This book focuses on the years 1831–1842, the crucial years when Lincoln, as a young man, was developing. Well-researched, giving insight into what helped to shape Lincoln.

Periodicals

Harold Holzer, "Lincoln's Early Years," *The New York Times,* February 8, 1998.

Joshua Kleinfield, "The Union Lincoln Made (Political and Legal Aspects of Writ of Habeas Corpus by President Lincoln During the Civil War)," *History Today,* vol. 47, November 1, 1997.

Peter Steinfels, "Beliefs (Lincoln was profoundly influenced by his family's religious faith although he did not share it)," *The New York Times,* February 19, 2000.

John M. Taylor, "Civil Rights an Early Casualty (Lincoln Measure Aimed at Secessionists in the North)," *The Washington Times,* December 8, 2001.

Documentaries

Abraham and Mary Lincoln: A House Divided, produced and directed by David Grubin, written by David Grubin and Geoffrey C. Ward, narrated by David McCullough. PBS (The American Experience), 2/19, 2/20, 2/21/2001.

Lincoln, produced and directed by Peter W. Kunhardt, written and produced by Phillip B. Kunhardt III and Phillip B. Kunhardt Jr., narrated by James Earl Jones. ABC, 12/26, 12/27/1992.

Index

Picture Credits

Cover photo: PhotoDisc

Courtesy of the Lincoln Museum, Fort Wayne, 12, 21, 29, 32, 36, 43, 48, 60, 69, 81, 95, 104

Library of Congress, 16, 19, 65, 75, 86, 93, 109, 111, 112

© Bettmann/CORBIS, 18, 54, 71, 92

Stock Montage, Inc., 23, 40

© CORBIS, 26, 44, 58, 68, 73, 76, 79, 96, 97, 101, 107, 113

Chris Jouan, 49, 63, 99

North Wind Picture Archives, 52, 89

About the Author

Karen Marie Graves holds a bachelor's degree in English literature and a master's degree in folklore and mythology, specializing in popular culture, from the University of California at Los Angeles. This is her second nonfiction book for young adults. She lives in California with her two children.